HUNTING
HOOLIGANS

HUNTING THE HOOLIGANS

THE INSIDE STORY OF OPERATION RED CARD

Michael Layton with Robert Endeacott

MILO BOOKS LTD

CONTENTS

Michael Layton served in both the British Transport Police and West Midlands Police, reaching the rank of chief superintendent, and headed numerous large-scale criminal investigations, including Operation Red Card. In 2003 he was awarded the Queen's Police Medal. He also served in the Sovereign Bases Police, in Cyprus, and is the author of the ebook *Violence in the Sun: A History of Football Hooliganism in Cyprus.*

Robert Endeacott is the author of numerous books including *Peaches: A Chronicle of the Stranglers*, *Dirty Leeds*, *Fanthology,* and *Disrepute: Revie's England.* He lives in Leeds.

AUTHORS' NOTE

OPERATION RED CARD was launched in 1987 to target the Zulu Warriors, a large hooligan gang that followed Birmingham City Football Club. Their name stemmed from an infamous confrontation in 1982 at Manchester City's Maine Road ground, during which rallying war cries of 'Zulu!' from the Birmingham contingent were frequently heard. The story soon passed into local folklore. It was a reference, of course, to the events portrayed in the film *Zulu*, set during the Anglo–Zulu War in 1879, when around a hundred and fifty British and colonial troops successfully defended the mission station at Rorke's Drift on the Tugela River, Natal Province, South Africa, against over four thousand native Zulu warriors. (Interestingly, Birmingham City FC had been created in 1875, just four years before the events depicted in the film, as Small Heath Alliance.) Operation Red Card would similarly see a small team of dedicated police officers assigned to take on a large number of determined, organised and ruthless individuals of various racial backgrounds. *This* group of officers would also be fiercely determined to win against immense odds.

The subject of football hooliganism has vexed the minds of the police service, governments and other agencies for decades.

Books and films, most of which have been told through the perspectives of hooligans, have provided an insight into this culture of organised violence. Its proponents frequently claim it is part of supporting a football team, but often it has very little to do with the sport. The archetypal football hooligan is a person who uses or exploits support for a team to indulge in or to promote violent or antisocial behaviour. It is a simple definition but one which has more complex aspects to it.

To use Birmingham City as a specific example, after every home game, large numbers of fans, including the hooligan element, would walk towards the city centre via such streets as Great Barr Street, Lower Dartmouth Street, Garrison Lane, Watery Lane with its large traffic island, Fazeley Street, Adderley Street, Lawley Street and Curzon Street. All of these streets had a history of public order incidents. They led to Albert Street and into the High Street area of the city centre, with wide thoroughfares ideal for skirmishes. The local police applied set-piece tactics to keep opposing fans apart but those plans became familiar to supporters, who often knew in advance exactly where the mounted police would be deployed. They frequently threw missiles at them as an aside.

Static police deployments would come under immense pressure as sometimes violence ebbed and flowed in different streets, whilst the Operational Support Units tried to maintain the flexibility to arrive in police transit vans if required. It was a complex mix where police tactics and resources were constantly tested and probed for weaknesses by hooligan elements. On arrival in the city centre, the Birmingham hooligans would conduct circuits, marching up the ramp at New

Street leading over the shopping centre, down via the steps and escalators to New Street Railway Station and on through the Bull Ring. Sometimes they would go via the Midland Red Bus Station too, through the indoor and outdoor markets, and back up towards the Rotunda building. The mob might take another sweep of New Street Station until moved out again by the British Transport Police. All of the time, they were looking to pick off and assault rival fans while playing cat-and-mouse with the police. They were cunning and sly and often very effective in their pursuit of violence. They had entirely separate tactics when travelling to away grounds to follow Birmingham City but it was still all about marking and defending 'territory' if it was your own, and successfully attacking someone else's if the opportunity arose. In animals, it is a matter of basic instinct and survival. In football hooligans, it was a matter of 'honour', respect and kudos.

In the 1980s, some UK police forces began to grade hooligans in their areas in three ways, namely A, B, and C. Category A hooligans might wear casual but fashionable clothes, have trendy hair styles, wear a small concealed club badge, be camera shy, operate in small groups, use hire cars or minibuses and be involved in planned violence. These hooligans were sometimes referred to as Casuals after their dress code and developed tactics born of experiences of being arrested. Category B hooligans might be more scruffy and slovenly, wear club colours, be exhibitionist, operate in large groups, use trains, coaches and private cars, and be involved in spontaneous violence. Category C might wear visible club colours, be easily led, might attach themselves to Category

B hooligans, use trains, coaches and private cars, and would possibly but not always get involved in violence.

Incorporating personal recollections of certain key personnel, including myself, and media reports, this book is the true story of how officers from the West Midlands Police declared war against the Zulu Warriors. It is not designed to be sensationalist or gratuitous, and it glorifies neither violence nor violent people, but is a genuine and honest account of disturbing times inextricably connected to English football. During the course of research for the book I managed to trace a number of former colleagues from the Special Operation Unit, many of whom I have not seen for more than twenty years. I was struck by their recall but also their collective pride in what was considered a job very well done. We had all taken different journeys in our careers and indeed in our personal lives but in respect of Operation Red Card there was still that common bond.

Michael Layton, QPM

IT'S NOT FOR me to comment on their quality, but so many stories have now been written about football hooliganism that it's often difficult to be sure which are authentic or even partly genuine. In fact some of the tales are about as credible as the accents in the shocking hooligan film Green Street! But one book I do not doubt the credentials of is Caroline Gall's Zulus: The Story of the Zulu Warriors Football Firm, which I found insightful and entertaining. I had decided to read it following a meeting I had with a former West Midlands police officer during research for another project I was working on at the time. That officer was Mike Layton, who it transpired was the man responsible for setting up the Birmingham task force to address the Blues' hooligan 'problem' of the Zulu Warriors. And that's how Mike and I came to collaborate on this book, the first ever, I believe, written from the angle of a police officer who led a successful anti-hooligan investigation: Operation Red Card (or Operation Rourke's Drift, to give it its original, misspelled name). I wanted to write about the subject using first-hand recollections from officers actually involved in the operation and incorporating witness accounts as well, all without prejudice or emotional attachment but definitely with a dramatic and emotive edge.

I was at the infamous Birmingham versus Leeds game in 1985, at City's St Andrew's ground, in the away supporters' section. And even though they didn't believe me – the bobbies and the St John Ambulance folk (who were brilliantly supportive) – the only violence I partook in was a cranial assault on a stadium girder lurking above my head as I foolishly jumped up to sit on a barrier. But I recall the whole afternoon being absolutely chaotic, with the St John's treatment room crammed with casualties and a long queue outside it waiting for treatment. All those in the room with me, being treated for a variety of injuries, seemed 'normal' and innocent, present on the day to watch a football match, not to fight or wage war on anyone.

Mayhem ruled that day in the West Midlands. Truthfully, many football followers of the era were used to such scenes – that isn't me condoning it, I'm just confirming it – but I would never have thought that any gangs like the Zulus really had the know-how to plan and organise hostilities so meticulously. As a football fan, you either chose to put up with the violence and the pervading atmosphere of aggression it brought, from opposing followers, from the police and sometimes even from your own team's supporters, or you stopped watching your team. I loved my football team too much to do that, and I'm glad of it, but nonetheless something had to be done. Too many innocent supporters were too often suffering through no fault of their own, and that is never right. Going to football matches frequently wasn't fun, it was like going to battle, and I am not trying to be righteous or pompous by saying that. Many followers, especially at away games, were herded like cattle by the police, and on the whole regarded with a similar low degree of respect by the government. The fact is that hooliganism was then as much a part of English football as an inadequate national team, badly treated fans and a misguided government that regarded many male fans as criminals guilty until proven innocent.

Robert Endeacott

PROLOGUE

CARDIFF TRAIN STATION, on a damp but fair Saturday afternoon, in September, 1972. Despite the relatively benign autumn weather, the day was not proving to be enjoyable. A football match was being played nearby and, even in 1972, the railway stations of the United Kingdom had the sinister potential to serve as warrens and lairs for the increasingly common beast known as the football hooligan. The Welsh capital's main station provided a prime location for violence if any soccer-following men desired it, and on that day, scores of them did: scores of Cardiff City fans intent on inflicting pain on the visiting Aston Villa supporters, who numbered only around one hundred. From the station concourse or an island platform, opposing fans could jeer, goad and threaten each other across the railway tracks to their bitter hearts' content. And on this day, the abuse had an added Welsh edge to it, a home-nation, next-door-neighbour nationalism.

Together with a few colleagues and the gathered Aston Villa followers, I stood as a nineteen-year-old British Transport Police (BTP) constable on a platform at Cardiff, preparing to escort a football train, or 'special', back to Birmingham. With me were a sergeant and three other constables. On the opposite platform, locals were beginning to congregate in small groups, emerging from subway steps and doorways, some of them waiting for their own trains to the Valleys and elsewhere, most of them waiting for something else. The Cardiff supporters numbered well over a hundred.

From their ranks a signal was suddenly shouted, followed immediately by a barrage of missiles thrown in almost perfect unison, a multitude of objects flying through the dimly lit air towards the Birmingham-bound crowd. Coins, glass bottles, drinks cans, marbles, metal nuts, bolts, stones and ball bearings bombarded the target area, along with a four-foot shunting pole with a metallic and dangerous hook on the end, now a makeshift spear. The visitors scattered and hid, and thankfully the shunting pole didn't hit anyone. That good fortune however didn't deter me from taking what in hindsight was possibly foolish action. Homing in on the Welsh spear thrower, I leapt off the platform and sprinted across the tracks to the opposite platform, somehow managing to make an arrest before the offender could even consider disengaging from the surrounding crowd or think of resisting. I bounded on to the platform, grabbed the scruffy, late-teens male and swiftly had him in an arm lock. With procedure, common sense and an impending train to Birmingham all prominent in my mind, I quickly guided the Cardiff lout down the steps to the subway to pass him on to local officers to deal with.

I had always hated violence. Thieving, I could understand but thuggery was a different matter. I saw no sense in such behaviour, perpetrated every week supposedly in the name of a sport. I was determined to show no quarter to those responsible and this philosophy stayed with me throughout my career. I simply would not tolerate anyone who tried to physically impose their will on others just because they were strong enough to do so, viewing it as a form of extreme cowardice.

I wasn't aware of it at the time but the stage was being set.

CHAPTER 1

THE ZULU WARRIORS

I ALREADY HAD a reputation as a thief taker when I joined the CID. A Brummie by birth, I was a police cadet from 1968 to August 1971, then for just over a year served as a constable with the British Transport Police in Birmingham. To an extent it was already in my blood: my father worked as a civilian enforcement officer with the law courts, was also a special constable, and was very supportive of my joining the police service. My initial training took place at the Home Office District Police Training Centre at Dishforth, in Yorkshire, where I received a book prize for being the top student in examinations. Because I was getting married and we wanted a police house, and the BTP was not able to provide such privileges, I transferred to Birmingham City Police in October 1972. I was posted in uniform for four years to Ladywood Police Station, which bordered the city centre, and spent part of that time working on the Theft From Vehicles Squad, where I developed a taste for dealing with 'lifestyle' criminals who stole cars as a way of life and used them to commit other crimes.

I had very little exposure to football. On one occasion a colleague took me to a Birmingham City match while we were out on observations on potential car thieves, and I was bored stiff. I saw nothing special about a bunch of grown men chasing after a ball. I was, however, fascinated by the crowd dynamics and the behaviour of people many of whom appeared to be out of their brains on drink.

I desperately wanted to transfer to the CID and work within a small team, and in August 1976, at the age of twenty-four, I made it, being appointed a detective constable at Ladywood. Two years later, I moved to Digbeth Police Station as uniform sergeant and a year after that I took over the management of a plain-clothes team known as the Digbeth Special Unit (DSU), tackling street crime in Birmingham city centre. This included robberies, burglaries, thefts of and from cars, shoplifting and purse snatching. It also gave me an opportunity to observe the various subcultures that frequented Birmingham city centre: skinheads, Mods, bikers, punks and others. They often didn't like each other, and fights would frequently ensue.

One particular pub seemed to be at the heart of much of my work. One summer evening in 1979, I arrested an absconder from a local approved school in The Crown, which was beside the main train station on the corner of Station Street and Hill Street. That July and August, I also investigated a serious wounding involving a group of skinheads who were rising to prominence in The Crown and its adjacent streets. Mods, rockers, punks and bikers were regulars on the scene too, and this meant frequent confrontations between rival groups in the city centre.

Normally public order problems were dealt with by officers in uniform but I decided that we needed to get up close to the trouble-causers, so we would stay in plain clothes. It was a risky strategy, opposed by some of my fellow supervisors, but I had great confidence in the team and our ability to control situations even if outnumbered. 'You are taking too many risks,' the other sergeants would say, but their words fell on deaf ears. Any arrests led to immediate handcuffing and we would frogmarch those arrested down to Digbeth Police Station, as it was quicker than waiting for a police car and avoided crowds gathering.

I was involved in countless rucks over the years but it was during this period that I was deliberately assaulted for the only time in my police career. One Saturday afternoon, I was out with three of the team in the outdoor markets area when we saw a group of long-haired rockers making their way towards the glass doors leading into the indoor market. We had already arrested two men for threatening behaviour nearby, and left one of the team in the station to deal with them. You could tell that there was tension in the air. As they were about to enter, some of the rockers jumped on a youth dressed as a Mod and started punching and kicking him. Everyone surged through the doors as the Mod tried to escape down some steps into the market, which was crammed with stalls and shoppers.

We ran after them. I burst through one set of doors and straight into the screaming mêlée, while my team ran through another set. In that instant we became separated but I imme-diately jumped on one of the attackers, shouting 'Police!' as loud as I could. He was having none of it and lashing out at me. We fell to the floor in the struggle and I hung on with him on top of me. The Mod took the opportunity to run off and now

I was the centre of attention, with boots flying. Fortunately my prisoner took most of the kicks. A Markets Police officer ran forward to help and was also assaulted. After what seemed an age the crowd parted and my team seemed to fly over the heads of the attackers. They made four more arrests as the rest scattered.

After a quick check-up at the General Hospital for bruising to my back, we processed the prisoners. Secretly I think the team felt guilty about the fact that I had got a kicking but it was not their fault and after some initial banter I chose not to give them a hard time over it. My attacker, a twenty-two-year-old from Quinton, got a month in prison and I suffered no lasting effects.

I was lucky. Being assaulted, whether you are a member of the public or a police officer, is the most personally invasive thing that can happen to you. Bruises and scars on the body will heal but scars in the mind may not. I had a close relative who was attacked in the street following a Birmingham City match, in an unprovoked incident. He never recovered from the experience and was deeply psychologically affected for the whole of his life, which no one could predict was ultimately to end in tragic circumstances. My experience was certainly nothing like that.

The DSU made scores of arrests for public order offences over a period of ten months. The shopping centres in the centre were also becoming the preserve of groups of youths of West Indian origin at the same time, but I remained absolutely confident that 'my gang' was as good as anyone else's, and remained clear that there would not be any no-go areas. As we moved around the shopping centres as a team, we would not give way to anyone obstructing the walkways. This was our territory.

*

On 11 March 1980, Chelsea visited Birmingham City to play an evening game. The Londoners were acquiring an appalling hooligan reputation of their own and in fighting involving skinheads in Station Street, near to The Crown, a young Chelsea fan was seriously wounded. There were also confrontations between Chelsea and local youths of West Indian descent in the shopping centres. I was on duty in one of my few experiences with football crowds, and as we mingled with Chelsea fans in the Birmingham Shopping Centre after the game, they started to get a bit lively. Some security staff moved in and I was bitten by one of their German shepherd dogs. A doctor at the Birmingham Accident Hospital later insisted I have a tetanus injection in a sensitive area, which was yet another dent to my pride.

Ten days later, happily recovered, I arrested an eighteen-year-old from Smethwick in The Crown for possession of a controlled drug. And a couple of months later, we made enquiries regarding a Section 47 assault by skinheads on a BTP officer at New Street Station, and subsequently arrested several shaven-headed teenagers. The lowest form of assault was known as a common assault, where normally no injuries were visible. The next one up was the Section 47, which generally involved evidence of minor cuts and bruises. A

Section 20 wounding was a more serious assault, with broken bones or knife injuries with no intent proved, and a Section 18 wounding was one below attempted murder but where a specific intent to cause the injuries was evidenced: for instance, a pre-planned attack. I remained fiercely loyal to my old force, and always did my best to help my former BTP colleagues. They were often referred to in somewhat disparaging terms as the 'railway police' by local officers, and somehow deemed to be not quite 'proper' police officers. It was not a view that I shared.

That June, racially fuelled clashes took place between white skinheads and black youths in the Small Heath district of the city, culminating in three arrests for public order offences on the following Saturday in Manzoni Gardens. The incidents arose out of recent National Front activity in Birmingham and London. On 23 August, with the new football season a week old, we arrested two more skinheads – one of them black – for threatening behaviour. They had confronted Manchester United fans in Digbeth before the match with Birmingham City. The interesting point for me is that white skinheads were taking on visiting football fans in the city centre while West Indian youths appeared to be operating independently, but at some point between 1980 and the game at Manchester City in 1982 they had begun to integrate, becoming the Zulu Warriors. And The Crown pub was clearly an integral part of the gang's beginning and emergence.

The Crown had once been a popular blues and rock venue, famous as the site of Black Sabbath's first ever gig and for hosting the likes of Led Zeppelin and Status Quo. But by the early 1980s it was overrun by skinheads, generally notorious for right-wing political beliefs ('beliefs' is possibly too generous a term, many just wanted someone to hate and foreigners and people of different skin colour were easy targets). We often visited the place to make arrests or follow up leads. Even though we were in plain clothes, they knew who we were but knew better than to openly challenge us. We always engaged them in small talk and banter but there were lines not to be crossed and they knew it. We knew their names and they knew ours, but our knowledge afforded us a degree of protection. If we didn't know who somebody was, we asked them and didn't take no for an answer. There were also public toilets outside and for a while the area became infamous for 'cottaging', so the pub grew popular with the gay community at about the same time. So the pub had a bizarre history of transition from blues freaks to rockers to skinheads to the gay community to the rise of the Zulu Warriors. It was one of several threads that would weave together to lead to Operation Red Card.

On 27 October 1980, I transferred to the CID at Steelhouse Lane as a detective sergeant. The office was a large, three-storey building with loads of character where 'Alex', who would work on Red Card with me, lived on the top floor in single men's quarters

ALEX: The rooms consisted of one wardrobe, one sink and one bed – that was it. My first experience of meeting 'Dogbreath', who was also on Red Card, was seeing him lounging around in his boxer shorts. It was not a pretty sight. Sometimes we used to hold morning parades in another officer's bedroom because he couldn't get up on time. The Inspector would have us standing around his bed holding our appointments (notebooks and truncheons) whilst he read out our postings. It was all very social and alcohol driven.

Whatever you see CID officers dealing with on the TV, I dealt with: cheque frauds, woundings, rapes, burglaries, vehicle crime, armed robberies and even murders. I was a stickler for detail and sometimes drove my team mad but I kept them safe from problems. I had no intention of following police officers who had done a sloppy job into the witness box at Crown Court.

In June 1981, I was heavily involved in a murder inquiry into the death of a taxi driver who had been attacked by a number of Hells Angels outside the Locarno Club in Hurst Street. Twenty-nine people were initially arrested, with more to follow. I was given the job of establishing a sequence of events and plotting the movements of all those involved through examining witness statements and prisoner interview records. It was all good experience for what was to come. Months later, I oversaw an investigation into a large brawl involving two separate factions of Iraqis on Aston University campus. My message to the local beat officer was to tell them that if they didn't desist they would all be arrested. They didn't and they were. I would be involved in another six murder cases over a four-year period.

In 1983, I met and cultivated my informant George – a pseudonym, of course. He was a godsend. He knew many

Birmingham football hooligans but, in spite of being a lifestyle or career criminal, he did not normally involve himself in violence. I first met him that summer; to be more accurate, I arrested him that summer, in Birmingham city centre. It was a street arrest and he fitted the description of someone circulated on police radio for an offence. Another CID officer and I were out and about in casual clothes owing to a rise in gangs stealing from shops and we grabbed him as he unwittingly hurried across a road towards us, out of breath and clearly trying to avoid detection.

Once he was in custody, it became clear that his fear of going to prison was greater than his fear of becoming an informant for me. I gave him a short time to think about it, even though he didn't know that I didn't actually have enough evidence to charge him, and despite the risks, he decided to 'sign up'. I would pay him on a results basis and whilst today it would probably be considered small money, £100 was a decent amount then. Informants run with the hare and the hounds but they know that if they get caught again committing crime they will not be spared by us. He routinely ran the risk of being discovered by the criminal fraternity as a 'grass' and I have no doubt that had he been caught then the consequences would have been severe. He knew this but lived with it and took the money I paid him. Nowadays he will probably be like me, with less hair and a bigger waistline, but he still deserves his anonymity, as his actions in aiding the police in the past would still be regarded as unforgivable in certain circles.

Through George, I got to know a lot about the activities of a large shoplifting team operating not just in the city centre but nationwide. They were well organised, more than forty-strong and came mostly from the 'E' Division. Among them was the target I referred to as Fats, who stood out in the crowd for pretty obvious reasons. Many of them also followed Birmingham City and became linked to Zulu activity. George was soon giving me job after job: I was in almost daily contact with him and my workload came almost entirely from his information. On one memorable occasion he 'put in' two full teams of criminals. Anything to do with informants had to be shown in red in your diary and mine started to show a lot of very positive red.

Another strand appeared when, in January 1984, I was making enquiries at an address about street robberies in a Birmingham shopping centre. The suspect's address was in Washwood Heath, Birmingham, and was the home of 'Francis', a black male of West Indian origin, stockily built and then eighteen years old, with short, black, curly hair. The enquiries drew a blank but Francis would go on to become our main target in Operation Red Card.

We were unaware of it at the time but Francis was an associate of the original leader of the first specifically organised semblance of the Zulu gang, a young black man nicknamed 'Cud', or 'Cuddles'. He would become even more prominent after the publication of the book Zulus, in which he features heavily, and would go on to run a successful security business in the city. Though we know the Zulu Warriors gang first 'arrived' on the hooligan scene at Manchester City in 1982, they were at that stage far from a well-drilled unit. It took over a year for such a process to commence, the probable turning point coming in late February 1984, when the Blues had won on the pitch against Tottenham Hotspur but were considered to have been effectively defeated off it. The consensus was that it was time for them to nominate a leader, someone to pull the gang's divided numbers together and make them a more efficient and therefore tougher gang. Cuddles was finally agreed upon to be that leader.

The Zulus effectively superseded a previous grouping, called The Apex, as the Birmingham City hooligan force. The Apex was effectively the first semi-organised Birmingham City hooligan mob but had no real hierarchy and no clear leader. Men from the Chelmsley Wood area of the city had dominated the Blues' terraces but Chelmsley Wood did not get on with the many other districts of the city. Chelmsley was the main 'mixed' firm, the others being mainly white. All these areas surrounded the city. It wasn't until a group of fifty or so black and white teenagers from areas such as Ladywood, Highgate, Bordesley Green, Lee Bank and Sparkbrook formed The Apex in the early eighties that the city centre became officially involved.

One of the most disturbing trends among this new breed was their contempt for the police uniform and a willingness to attack and injure officers without compunction. In May 1984, a policeman was wounded following the Birmingham City game against Southampton at St Andrew's, a game which saw City relegated from the First to the Second Division. PC Andrew Thomas, aged thirty, was helping to escort more than 1,000 supporters outside the ground when some broke free, turned over a police van and attacked him. He was hit on the head by a brick and punched and kicked by a gang. 'I grappled with one lad and then saw stars and collapsed,' he later recalled. 'I looked up and saw about fifteen fans putting the boot in as I lay on the ground. Words alone cannot describe how I feel. I was treated like a punchbag. I shall be scarred for life and I ache from bruises all over my body.' A lone Blues fan who tried to protect him was also beaten up for his trouble and they both finished up in East Birmingham Hospital, where the officer had eleven stitches in his wounds. Twenty-six people were arrested but none for the assault on the officer.

I saw my informant George two days later and he named a twenty-year-old suspect who we managed to arrest on the Wednesday in Bordesley Green. This suspect denied the offence and so was police bailed. It was frustrating but you could hardly tell the prisoner why you knew what he had been up to. We learned that he was close to an individual we would nickname 'Cab' who would later become a target of ours and who mixed with the Bordesley crew, many of whom also became Zulu Warriors. Cab was of West Indian extraction, around seventeen years old, from Bordesley Green. He had black curly hair, big eyebrows and a slight moustache and was outwardly a quiet individual, but it would become evident that he was scared of no one.

While I had little direct experience of policing football, I was well aware of the violent atmosphere of the time around matches, as recounted here by a former colleague of mine who wishes to remain anonymous. I shall call him Neil:

SERGEANT NEIL: I policed numerous football matches in Birmingham in the late seventies and early eighties. This was before the real advent of CCTV, and crowd trouble particularly after the match around the grounds was a weekly occurrence. At that time, all the teams in the West Midlands Police area were in the old First Division, so every week you would have a big team from London or from up North visiting either Wolves, Coventry, Albion, Villa or Blues. They weren't coming just for the football. This was tribal and an encroachment on someone else's turf, resulting quite often in some ugly acts of violence.

Teams on their way to matches in other parts of the country used to stop off in Birmingham for a 'knock'. One Saturday afternoon the Inter City Firm, named after the British Rail trains at the time, from West Ham got off at New Street Station, ran into the shopping centre shouting 'ICF', smashed a load of shop windows and ran back down onto the station and disappeared on the next train out. On another occasion Villa fans visiting Nottingham 'did over' a flash menswear shop on their way home. After the police in Birmingham were notified, we simply stood on the platform at Birmingham New Street to await the returning football special. We arrested eight fans wearing brand new sheepskin coats as they swaggered down the platform like a bunch of Del Boys.

It would be common after a big match to have fifty to sixty prisoners from the day waiting to be processed at the police station nearest the ground. On one occasion we even detained a couple of coachloads of Chelsea fans after a stabbing. 'Facking hell, John, the Old Bill are taking us into the facking nick,' one fan was heard to remark.

Some time later, I joined the uniform support unit that used to police these matches full-time. The team was made up of a sergeant and eight PCs and travelled around in a liveried Ford Transit. Along with other, similar units, our job was to get to any trouble as quickly as possible and sort it out, which basically meant arresting anyone committing a public order offence. The silly thing was, even when we turned up, they would keep fighting as though we weren't there. I don't know how such incidents were policed in the rest of the country but in Birmingham it was zero tolerance.

Looking back, I can't believe what it was like at times. I remember once going over to the Molineux where Wolves were about to play Chelsea. It was 12.30 and the match was due to kick off at 3 p.m. When we got there, we immediately received a call to divert to Wolverhampton city centre as there was trouble – and how! A trainload of Chelsea fans had arrived early and were running amok. This continued throughout the match and after the final whistle. I took three men into custody that afternoon, it was so bad.

At the age of thirty-two, after eighteen months on the Support Unit and with six years' service, I was promoted to sergeant and posted to Birmingham city centre. Again I had numerous dealings with football fans, mostly from Villa and Birmingham City. Coming from Liverpool, I wasn't a supporter of either team. The Redmen from my home city were winning everything in sight at that time so I was happy.

However, I couldn't believe the animosity between Villa and Birmingham fans. There was real hatred. I visited both grounds on numerous occasions. Villa Park was much bigger, affluent and always in a stage of redevelopment. St Andrew's, the home of the Blues, could best be described as a tip at that time; one of the most desolate, scruffy, windy grounds I had ever visited. It was also very strange. Each corner of the ground had a crucifix attached to the floodlight pylon. Apparently the ground had been cursed years earlier and one of the managers had decided to place them there for good luck. It didn't work. Birmingham as a football team were abysmal.

The home fans were very strange as well. Instead of congregating at one of the goal mouth ends to cheer on their team like most fans at other grounds, they instead stood in line with the halfway line. Very odd. Their idea of providing refreshments at the ground was a kid walking round pitch-side with what can only be described as a large water tank strapped to his back. Protruding from this was a length of rigid copper pipe with a tap which was in such a position that the lad could dispense tea to the first few rows of the crowd – in plastic cups, I hasten to add. Mind you they could have just opened their mouths and he could have turned the tap on and left it running.

At my football ground, I was used to Gerry Marsden and the crowd singing 'You'll Never Walk Alone', a feelgood song that still makes the hairs on the back of my neck stand on end. Birmingham City also had a song, 'Keep Right On to the End of the Road', made famous by a long-gone music hall entertainer. This was adopted by the fans to commemorate their one and only taste of European football, years previously in some former Yugoslav city, which ended in failure. This is always sung by the fans when they subsequently fail. It's a song about never really getting there and it just about sums up the whole set-up.

Some of the younger fans were known as Zulu Warriors. Why they were called that, I have no idea. Any trouble involving these fans and the chant of 'Zulu, Zulu' went up. In the early days, my opinion was that these were just kids having a bit of a scuffle. However, as the years went on their numbers and acts of violence increased. The aggravation could also break out without a football match taking place. There were some reports of Zulu Warriors being responsible for some nasty stabbings and people being glassed in pubs. They were also notorious on their away trips.

CHAPTER 2

THE LEEDS RIOT

COUNTLESS INCIDENTS OF mayhem blighted English football grounds and their environs in the late twentieth century. Many of these incidents prompted police action and were reported by the media, and a large number were statistically recorded by the authorities. Football followers were wounded, even killed, at matches, while stadiums were wrecked and private property was trashed, all in the name of sports tribalism. And because of the seemingly spontaneous and 'unplanned' nature of these offences, committed by random individuals and gangs, the police and authorities were only ever able to react to situations rather than be proactive. By the late 1970s, the hooliganism, publicised by media sensationalism if not near hysteria, had become so bad that it was hitting match attendances. Dwindling crowds signified less income for the football clubs and, in professional sport, declining gate receipts is a mortal illness.

The situation continued alarmingly into the 1980s. Gates fell as many supporters, particularly the more elderly, were deterred by the evil atmosphere at many games and the constant air of menace. While most football clubs in the English

Football League were blessed with passionate followers who showed amazing devotion to their team, too many now were taking their fanaticism to disturbing lengths. By the start of the 1984–85 season, which would come to mark something of a turning point in official attitudes towards the game and its spectators, hooliganism was endemic. The participants had organised themselves into named, identifiable gangs and their levels of organisation and sophistication were worryingly impressive. And for Birmingham City, relegation that season to Division Two meant new grounds and towns to visit and the opportunity to lord it over smaller clubs with weaker support.

Their very first game of the season, on 25 August, brought a foretaste of what to expect, as one local newspaper later reported:

Violence marred the first day of the new soccer season with the arrest of Midlands fans. Ten Birmingham City fans will be appearing at court in Oldham after trouble flared at Blues' first match in the Second Division at Oldham Athletic on Saturday. Stones were thrown at police and rival supporters as around 300 Blues fans forced their way in to the ground through one of the main gates. Three policemen, one a chief inspector, were injured in the stone-throwing barrage which followed. One of the injured policemen was taken to hospital. One officer said later, 'It was just like the miners' picket, at the ground.' A 20-year-old Birmingham man has been charged with wounding a police officer. A further sixteen fans, ten from the Midlands, were arrested and later charged with Public Order offences. The fans caused further trouble when they

*left the ground, on the rampage through streets. When Blues
fans got home, violence flared once more as they fought with
youths in the city centre of Birmingham after leaving New
Street Train Station. Police stepped in and made nine arrests.
The same day, 17 arrests were made before and after the game
at Villa Park between Aston Villa and Coventry City and 14
arrests at Wolverhampton following Wanderers' game with
Sheffield United.*

Twelve years after my initial taste of soccer yobbery at Cardiff
Station in 1972, I found myself on another platform in another
station in another city, facing the same scenario. Saturday,
13 October 1984, would be unlucky thirteen for some. It was
late afternoon and Birmingham New Street Station's insipid
lighting was fighting a losing battle with the deepening darkness. A robust example of pioneering architecture and design
– for the 1960s at least – the station was a concrete and steel
eyesore, like much of a city centre where pedestrians' rights
came second to those of motorists. And to think that the city
Coat of Arms bears the motto 'Forward'!

In the history of Birmingham, when the architects and the
town planners have got it right the cityscape and the skyline
have been blessed with visionary style and grace. Even the
Rotunda building, that peculiar, futuristic tube-shaped crea-
tion belonging to a Captain Scarlet backdrop, has a certain
appeal. But when they have failed in their designs, sights more
befitting Kubrick's A Clockwork Orange have been dumped
on the place. This was one of those examples. The station
concourse, its walls ingrained with years of grime and its

beige flooring no longer shiny but dull, damp, sticky and ugly, pained the sensibilities of everyone unlucky enough to be there. Cigarette butts, gum, litter, spillages, the detritus of the couldn't-give-a-damns, made it filthier, uglier. Areas smelt of diesel fumes, tobacco smoke, even urine. And on Saturdays, the station's busiest day, an air of indifference, even unfriendliness, abounded.

To my left were public telephones, plastic seating and large pillars useful for people to hide behind if that way inclined. On football match days, youths and men are that way inclined. To the right were kiosks, a newsagent's, a travel agency, more pillars. In the centre, escalators rose to the Pallasades Shopping Centre, a network of retail outlets housed under one roof. Here was a ticket barrier, surly ticket inspectors, a ticket machine on the wall. Past the barrier, it was darker, grimmer. An overhead footbridge connected the station's twelve platforms, a slummy bar and even slummier public conveniences.

For reasons of personal safety, Birmingham New Street Station was best avoided on match days. For thousands of regular commuters, however, it was unavoidable: thousands of normal people leaving, thousands of normal people arriving, most with no interest in football or fighting. Disturbingly, the throng was about to increase in size, in intensity and in menace: hundreds of football spectators were due to arrive after walking from the St Andrew's stadium, followers of Birmingham City FC. In front of them were fans of Blackburn Rovers FC. The snake of Lancastrians was accompanied by a police escort and trailed by the City mob, through Digbeth with its decrepit factories and warehouses and its relic of a high street. Three police transit vans brought up the rear. There were more Birmingham hooligans present than Blackburn fans and police combined.

When things are going smoothly from a police perspective, away supporters are swiftly and proficiently passed on to the attendant officers of British Transport Police (BTP) to handle, taken through the ticket barrier and down to the station platforms to board their respective train. If things are not going smoothly, the away supporters are made to wait on the concourse, with a ring of police officers surrounding them either as a protective measure or a preventative one, depending on which football team is involved and how aggressive their followers are. Today's visitors, Blackburn Rovers, had beaten Birmingham City 2–0. Unsurprisingly, this had not gone down well with the home support and around three hundred of them were at the station to bid a special brand of farewell to the visitors. Their team had triumphed on the pitch but there was no chance of a Blackburn victory off the field of play, not when the Zulu Warriors were involved and especially when on home territory.

On the concourse, from one section of the many unescorted Birmingham City males, guttural chants of 'Zulu' rose, alarming and instilling fear in many of the innocent passersby. A series of assaults quickly followed: on Blackburn fans, on police officers and on railway personnel. Two BTP officers were hurt and the beige flooring was soon speckled with traces of their blood from face wounds. Yet only one person was arrested, and later charged with affray, good odds for the mob of 300 to 1. With the relatively small numbers of BTP officers on duty, and the fact that every prisoner took two officers off the streets for several hours to deal with them, this was probably as good as it was going to get.

The Zulu Warriors ruled the place. They ruled the football ground, they ruled New Street Station and they ruled Birmingham city centre. Unofficially, of course. The authorities did not recognise the Zulus' influence yet. For now it was a slow-burning matter. But before long it would ignite, indeed explode. And eventually I would be given the responsibility of leading the firefight.

Ten days later, in the evening, I met by arrangement my informant George, picking him up off the street in one of the plain CID cars. I parked up somewhere quiet. As I listened to him talk and caught up on what was going on, I heard about the Blackburn events and that attack on the BTP officers. He confirmed the presence of faces from the Bordesley Green and Stechford 'crew', who regularly engaged in organised shoplifting in the city centre and who were also members of the Zulu Warriors, a gang I knew had been involved in numerous affrays.

George was by then a long-standing informant of mine, which was somewhat unusual. Even today I feel the need to ensure that I protect his identity. It is part of the code and without it you cannot build the trust that is crucial to the process. Like many informants, he had found himself in a situation where initially he needed me more than he needed his friends; the possibility of facing prison was too much for him. I make no excuses for preying on that fear in a precise and calculating manner; he was not doing this out of a sense of public duty, he was surviving in the best way he thought he could, while I was deliberately narrowing his options.

At times he gave me so much information that I couldn't keep up with arresting all of the people he put in. As our relationship grew, I believe that he started to enjoy the adrenalin rush that came with the secret meetings and the ever-present fear of exposure. One false move or wrong word would have placed him in serious danger but he was up for it and proved to be invaluable on many occasions. Informants save the police huge amounts of money in time and effort and it was good to have him on my side. I knew instinctively from working with other informants that there would be a day when we would part company but it was not to be yet, and we enjoyed a few pints in dark and strange corners of rough pubs for some time to come. We were never friends but the reality was that I often spent more time with him than I did with my family.

George's revelations planted a seed in my mind. Something had to be done about the Zulu Warriors. But what, exactly? And how?

*

The last game of that 1984–85 league season was on a Saturday, 11 May. Birmingham City had already gained promotion for the following season to Division One, which in those pre-Premier League days was the top tier of English football, and were playing at their home ground, St Andrew's. The visitors, Leeds United, themselves had a slight chance of promotion too, providing they won this match and certain other results went their way too. So you might think that both teams' followers would be focused on the football to come, and that for the Blues fans at least it would be a day of celebration. You would be badly wrong.

Steve Burrows was a police constable on duty that day. He later worked for me.

STEVE BURROWS: I was still in my probation with about five months to go. I regularly performed duty at the Blues and my abiding memory is that it was the coldest I had ever been. The joke was that there was nothing between St Andrew's and the Ural Mountains and much of a match was spent taking turns warming up in the air from the outlet vent on the hot dog stand.

A couple of days before the match I was sent to Sheldon Police Station to pick up some paperwork. I bumped into the Football Intelligence Officer, who asked me if I was at the match on Saturday. He then told me that there was going to be trouble, as they had heard that the Leeds fans were going to try to stop the match if their team was losing. He then delighted in telling me that 'the gaffers' didn't believe the intelligence and, ever cost conscious, had decided not to put extra cops on duty, especially as they were expecting trouble at the WBA v Arsenal match a few miles away and had deployed the Operational Support Unit there. Of course he wasn't on duty at the match himself!

So it was that I found myself sat in the Railway End stand at St Andrew's for match briefing, looking around at a few score officers scattered in the seats and thinking that this could be an interesting afternoon.

Many Leeds fans arriving early by train had left the station to drink in nearby pubs. Well before kick-off, the Zulu Warriors

attacked around thirty away supporters, as well as a dozen or
so regulars, drinking in the Australian Bar, in Hurst Street, a
few hundred yards from New Street Station. Under the Zulu
umbrella existed a number of distinct groups with their own
specific nicknames, such as the 'Sauce Force', 'Brew Crew'
and the more widely known 'Junior Business Boys'. The
latter totalled around sixty youths who were younger than
the others, usually aged from fourteen to seventeen years. In
preparation for the visit of Leeds, the Junior Business Boys
were supposedly 'tooled up' with weapons and had been
actively looking for their rivals. Frustrated at not being able
to coax the visitors out of the Australian Bar, and hearing 'We
are Leeds' chants from inside, they began throwing objects
at the pub windows. The wife of the bar's landlord later
described how one man ran into the pub to shout a warning
just before the Birmingham yobs attacked. 'There were a
hundred and fifty to two hundred in the street,' she said.
'Some carried stools out and then threw them back in. Some
ran in and took out tables. It all happened in ten minutes.' The
pub's exterior windows were smashed, causing several thousand pounds' worth of damage. Some injuries were reported,
none of them major.

At the stadium, the Leeds fans, estimated at around 6,000,
were housed in the Tilton Road corner section, effectively
caged in behind twelve-foot fencing. However, it became
disturbingly apparent that the allocated space was insufficient
and that, with too many people crammed into too small a
place, people could be crushed to death. Mercifully the police
set about opening the adjoining, empty section to relieve the

pressure. Of those 6,000 Leeds followers, police estimates showed that some 500 were intent on causing trouble.

STEVE BURROWS: I took up duty on the touchline at the Railway End. This was where the Family Enclosure was situated, in which rosy cheeked young Blues fans could come with their parents in safety to follow the generally depressing fortunes of Birmingham City. Thus there was no fence at this end of the ground. The visiting fans' end had a full security fence and this is where the Leeds fans were to be imprisoned for the match and for some time afterwards.

Things didn't look good right from the start. When I took up position there were already several thousand Leeds fans in the ground and they were not happy. They had an awful reputation and lived up to it that afternoon. They were throwing missiles and then proceeded to remove the roof from the hot dog stand and throw it over the fence. Still at least they were fenced in.

As I viewed the gathering crowd in the Railway End, I started to spot familiar faces; not excited youngsters but a selection of local troublemakers with whom I regularly crossed swords who were members of the infamous Zulu Warriors. It gradually dawned upon me that they had somehow managed to plan their way into the Railway End where there was no fence. To this day I believe that the day's events were orchestrated between the Zulu Warriors and the Leeds fans in advance.

The first pitch invasion came at half-time and came from the Railway End. In the light of what came later, this was I suppose a minor skirmish but half-time was a lengthy affair accompanied by missiles and some robust policing that eventually restored order. That was the lull before the storm.

At 5.17 p.m., the final whistle of the match was blown. Birmingham hooligans, armed with broken plastic seating, parts of advertisement hoardings, iron stanchions, pieces of wood, glass bottles and even a large kettle, teemed onto the pitch towards the Leeds section, attacking more than a hundred policemen, including seven mounted officers, who stood in their way. The horses were targets too. Within seconds, the police were struggling at both ends of the pitch. Some St Andrew's match stewards who normally held keys to unlock the exit gates at the end of a game were said to have fled as they were attacked by home fans. One police officer was dragged into the Birmingham crowd and severely beaten. Several horses were injured, the worst being a fifteen-year-old bay gelding called Hidalgo, which suffered deep cuts to its legs when pulled down onto the concrete outside the ground. Several of the mounted officers were also hurt. PC Steve Gwilt was struck in the face with a four-foot piece of wood and had to be detained in hospital and Sergeant John Fitzmaurice suffered a broken nose, while five others had broken hand bones, fractured ribs or cracked kneecaps.

Birmingham City manager Ron Saunders was summoned and at 5.20 p.m. made a despairing appeal over the stadium public address system, asking the crowd to go home. Now penned in one corner, many of the thugs responded with another charge towards the police, counter-attacking and throwing missiles at them, causing the alarmed horses to buck and rear up. Saunders' voice again came across the airwaves – 'In the name of football, please stop' – and the violence did gradually subside, but it needed actions rather than strong words to have an effect: a final police charge, led by the 'cavalry', helped to scatter the mob and curtail the riot. Even then, a flare was fired at the thin blue line of mounted police. Inspector Des Turner, who led the baton charge, said, 'Luckily it just missed us and landed harmlessly on the ground, but if the idiot who fired the gun had slipped and the flare had gone into the stands then we could easily have had another Bradford on our hands. I have covered hundreds of games but I have never seen one like this. It really frightened me and was sheer, irresponsible madness.'

STEVE BURROWS: The second invasion involved hundreds of youths, all Birmingham 'fans' and all from the Railway End. Seats were ripped up and skimmed as missiles. I recall being hit on the arm by one and it was thrown from such close range I saw who did it. Being a resourceful cop I found the goal quite useful to shelter in. I probably spent more time in it than the ball that season. One of my clearest memories was the sergeant in charge of my section running along the touchline shouting, 'That's it lads, fuck Plan A and Plan B, it's Plan C: every man for themselves!'

The irony was that the other end was by now policed by the OSU in full riot gear, who had been diverted from the Albion match at half-time. They had the fence on their side and if you watch the film of the trouble they can be seen discouraging the Leeds fans from climbing the fence with as good a display of synchronised truncheoning as ever seen on video. I don't think any Leeds fans got over that fence.

At the other end we had no riot gear, 'tit hats' on, no shields, wooden truncheons and no fence. The battle lines ebbed back and forth and at one stage I was nearly in the centre tunnel, thinking that if we got backed into there we would get a good hiding. The day was saved by the horses. It was like the Charge of the Light Brigade, especially the white horse who continually rode backwards and forwards knocking the hooligans over like ninepins.

Encouraged by this we formed into a line with 'pegs' drawn and mounted a ferocious charge. The ACC was next to me laying about him like a good 'un and on a positive note I came across the seat thrower from earlier who did not enjoy our reunion. We finally beat the invaders back into the seats and I can remember a number of them being hauled up onto the upper tier by others in order to escape due process (i.e. a clout with a truncheon). Finally the ground was clear bar the Leeds fans penned behind their fence.

Two officers who would both play important roles in Operation Red Card's final stages, Bryan Dorrian and Ian Mabbett, had well-informed perspectives on the riot and on the Birmingham hooligan scene of that time. Bryan would later retire as a detective constable after forty-three years with West Midlands Police and the BTP and is an expert in mobile surveillance. Ian Mabbett was in the Criminal Investigation Department (CID) with the BTP in Birmingham at the time of the riot.

BRYAN DORRIAN: I am a lifelong Birmingham City supporter and used to follow them with my father and uncle. When I was a police cadet, our football trainer was Keith Norman, an ex-Aston Villa player, who encouraged me. I was actually signed with the Villa youth team for two seasons but Brian Little was the only one who really made it from my era. In my time I suffered two broken legs so I decided to join the police, as a regular officer. I was off duty in the main stand seating area for the game. I remember the mounted police officer on the white horse on the pitch and Leeds fans trying to get at Blues fans in the bottom corner of the Spion Kop area. There just weren't enough police officers there and I left as soon as it was safe. As a football fan I have always been quite sad about why they turn to violence. I am also a keen rugby fan and have been to international games. I have never seen the same level of violence and usually you can go to a game, have a drink and just talk about sport.

IAN MABBETT: I have always been mad for football and was born a Blues fan. I was a season ticket holder and my dad took me to the ground as a ten-year-old. And I did the same with my son. I was on holiday for the Blues–Leeds Riot in 1985 but he was there and told me it was terrible. There were regular chants of 'Zulu! Zulu!' in the ground and they used to run up and down the aisles but a lot of people were hangers-on, not proper Zulus. It was noticeable over a period of time how more black lads became involved. Initially they were predominantly white.

The worst was to come. In a terrible incident soon after the match, a young Leeds fan was killed by a long section of wall collapsing and crashing down on him in the away part of the stadium. Ian Hanbridge, aged fifteen, was reportedly attending his first ever professional football match. An ambulance belonging to the voluntary organisation St John Ambulance was attacked with bricks, while stones were thrown at individual St John volunteers, with at least a dozen of them suffering injuries as a result. One, nineteen-year-old Diane Buckle, later told the press, 'I was checking a Leeds fan for leg injuries shortly after the wall collapsed when a Birmingham fan came over and started trying to kick him. The fan was very drunk so I told him to sit down but then one of his kicks caught me under the ribs. When I stood up, I just passed out.' Also, outside the ground, a gang of 200 Leeds fans attacked a coach carrying Birmingham guests back from an Indian wedding; most of the windows were smashed. The coach was pelted with bricks, five people inside were injured and others, including a disabled pensioner, needed treatment for shock.

There would be more than one hundred arrests, about half of them made retrospectively. More than five hundred people were injured, including at least a hundred police officers.

STEVE BURROWS: We were formed up on the centre circle by the Chief Inspector who praised us then gave the unwelcome news that trouble outside the ground needed sorting out and we were the ones to do it. There were about thirty of us, I guess, none of us having any riot gear. We exited the ground into Garrison Lane. In those days you came out onto a road that led to a children's playground, set at a much lower level, that was invisible from where we were standing. About 100 yards away we could see thirty or forty 'scufflers' milling about and the chief inspector decided that a charge would be appropriate. We formed into a line, drew our pegs and, with a blood-curdling cry, off we went. As we got closer, the hooligans began disappearing out of sight down the drop into the playground.

Encouraged by this success, our momentum increased, fuelled by a touch of red mist – it had been a long day by then. As we drew closer, the playground, a large tarmacked area, began to become visible. I was right next to the CI and I can remember shouting, 'Gaffer, gaffer, can you see what's down there?' He was in full charge mode but eventually realised that the playground was occupied by several hundred youths busily ripping the swings out of the ground to use as weapons. As we appeared a primeval roar went up and, as one, we skidded to a halt at the edge of the drop. The CI shouted in true Monty Python fashion: 'Fuck me, right lads, run away,' and we retraced our charge at about the same speed. Our pursuers stopped to turn over a police van, which probably saved us, as reinforcements arrived in the form of a load of 'scruffies' (police motorcyclists), having the advantage of crash helmets and full leathers. As luck would have it, the overturned van belonged to the OSU and was full of shields, which we liberated and then we joined our rescuers in chasing off the crowd.

I can remember having to walk from the ground into Birmingham city centre chasing Zulus, finally finishing at about 7.30 pm with a bruised arm and enough war stories to last for the next few months. When I got home I expected to have been part of big news but of course it was the same day as the Bradford fire disaster which, together with the tragic death of a lad when a wall collapsed at St Andrew's, rightly overshadowed my part in the Blues–Leeds riot.

The Birmingham mobs streamed back through Digbeth into the city centre, throwing bricks at passing cars and at any police too, with another officer being felled by one of the projectiles. In the city centre, gangs looted shops. At one menswear store, the mob managed to smash a reinforced window and snatched suede and leather coats valued at up to £15,000.

More than one hundred and twenty-five people were arrested on the day. Three Birmingham hospitals went on to full alert. Forty people were treated at East Birmingham Hospital with six being detained. Another thirty-five were treated at Birmingham Accident Hospital and again, six were detained. Fourteen people were treated at the General Hospital. Ninety-six officers needed hospital treatment, with twelve of them detained, including PC Michael Corrigan of the Operational Support Unit (OSU) with back and foot injuries. He was hurt when the twelve-foot-high wall above an exit collapsed under crowd pressure in the terrible incident in which young Ian Hanbridge died. 'There were some fans who were marvellous,' PC Corrigan later told a reporter. 'They helped shift bricks to get us free and the St John Ambulance did a great job.' Officials at St Andrew's later estimated the value of the damage at more than

£30,000. It included a burnt-out refreshment bar and eight cars which were wrecked and later stripped of parts by thieves. Further damage of £2,000 was caused to St John Ambulance equipment.

That Saturday I was off duty on a 'weekly leave day', doing nothing special and, unlike many of my colleagues, had no interest in the match at St Andrew's. I hated the game of football, and nothing I have seen over the years has persuaded me to change my opinion. I was at the time a detective sergeant working on the Force Surveillance Unit. It was a posting that I was eminently unsuitable for and I couldn't wait to leave and get back to the CID work that I knew well. The reality was that I was existing in a part of the twilight world of policing which requires extremely high levels of technical expertise and professionalism but can also be profoundly boring, as you spend hour after hour in uncomfortable situations waiting for something that might never happen. The events at St Andrew's had no impact on my policing role at the time, though I did find the scenes on television disturbing. One local newspaper headline consequently proclaimed, 'Fans batter cops in big riot.' We, the police, had not won that day, indeed there were no winners, and I didn't like it. It felt personal.

On any 'normal' day, the scenes at St Andrew's would have shocked and disgusted people all around the world. However, even more horrifying events in West Yorkshire overshadowed the Birmingham disgrace. That same, fateful afternoon, more than fifty people died and more than a hundred were seriously injured when the main stand burnt down at Bradford City's Valley Parade stadium. In a matter of minutes the stand turned into a hellish inferno, destroying the building and ruining countless lives.

Shadow Sports Minister Mr Denis Howell MP was at the Birmingham–Leeds match. He would claim that the National Front was actively using clubs like Birmingham City and Aston Villa as recruiting grounds for racially motivated violence and that fan groups from West Ham, Chelsea and Leeds had also been infiltrated. He also alluded to the hard-line hooligan element on the day of the riot, known as the Leeds Service Crew, who were, he said, backed by a violent group known as 'The Trendies' because they wore expensive tracksuits and leisure wear stolen from shops. He remarked that he had no doubt that the riot was a concerted attack on the law, order and peace of England's society.

Within weeks, events unfolded which, improbably, shocked and sickened the world even more. Following violent confrontations between opposing supporters, escaping fans were pressed against a wall and barriers in the Heysel Stadium in Brussels, Belgium, before the start of the 1985 European Cup Final between Liverpool FC and Juventus of Italy on 29 May. Thirty-nine people, most of them Juventus fans, died and six hundred more were injured.

An eminent judge, Oliver Popplewell, had been appointed to chair an inquiry into the events at Bradford and Birmingham. Subsequently it was felt that his remit was wide enough to cover the circumstances of the Heysel disaster too, and he was chosen to chair a full-blown Committee of Inquiry into Crowd Safety at Sports Grounds. The interim report of what became known as the Popplewell Committee considered that unless the hooligan problem was addressed 'football may not be able to continue in its present form much longer' and thus club membership schemes started to be debated. Mr Justice Popplewell said of the Birmingham–Leeds game that it was 'more like the Battle of Agincourt than a football match'.

Those awful events of May 1985 would have given any reasonable person pause for thought. Yet incredibly the following season saw little let-up in the mayhem.

CHAPTER 3

A GATHERING STORM

IN EARLY AUGUST, 1985, Birmingham City played a so-called friendly match at Port Vale, in Staffordshire, before the start of the new season. A number of Blues supporters travelled by train to Longport, a few miles from Port Vale, probably in an attempt to avoid police attention. After the game, they slyly tested police cordons during face-offs with local fans, while chanting 'Zulu!' It had the feel of a dry-run before the start of the main event. Port Vale were viewed as small fry by the Brummies, for whom promotion back to Division One meant choice clashes would once again be on offer against the country's biggest 'firms'. The Zulus were keen to make their mark. Interestingly, according to the book Zulus it would be early in this new football season that the gang effectively split into two, with Cuddles leading the main group, who were almost exclusively into fighting, while his sidekick 'Wally' would head a more criminally minded group who often used football as a cover for stealing and robbery.

On 13 August, Birmingham City hosted West Ham United for an 11.30 a.m. kick-off. Large numbers of home supporters gathered in Birmingham city centre after the game, specifically around the concourse of New Street Railway Station. With 'Zulu' chants again filling the air, they clashed violently with West Ham hooligans and the police struggled to keep the two sides apart, despite the deployment of dogs to help the officers.

Blues were in London to play Chelsea on 24 August. It was another big day for the trouble-minded. Chelsea, like West Ham, were well known for having a sizeable number of thugs in their ranks, many of them racist or, politely speaking, politically right-wing, something which riled the multi-racial Zulu Warriors. Hundreds of the Midlands gang made the trip, many of them by train. The waiting police escorted some of them to Tottenham Court Road but then left them to their own devices, perhaps a seemingly pointless tactic but one which generally does help to preserve order.

The straightforward truth is that the local police forces of England would much prefer a complete ban on all away supporters, an entirely understandable preference as it would make their jobs a lot easier and enable them to concentrate on 'real' crime as well as saving the country large amounts of money. With its huge open concourse, on any day Euston Station is a major challenge to police and to control but on match days it is beyond challenging, it is a near impossibility. The easy access to the Underground from Euston helps the hooligan elements by enabling them to move swiftly and unsupervised from one place to another in large numbers. Such large and potentially unruly crowds create an extremely frightening and intimidating experience for the public, especially on the Underground.

Scores of Birmingham followers journeyed to London from the West Midlands by coach too, arriving at Victoria Coach Station, where they were able to congregate with fellow 'Bluenoses' already in London. Eventually a group of some three hundred began walking to the football ground, Stamford Bridge. Chelsea hooligans were waiting for them at a nearby wine bar, but they weren't there to share a glass of Chardonnay. When spotted, both sets charged at each other and the main front window of the wine bar was smashed. Somewhat surprisingly, no serious injuries were reported.

At 11.20 p.m. on Friday, 6 September, on the eve of a derby match, around twenty black youths forced their way into the Old Contemptibles pub in Edmund Street, Birmingham city centre, armed with bricks and other missiles and chanting, 'Zulu!' The Old Contemptibles was known to be a Villa pub, frequented by their fans. Aston Villa, from the Aston area of Birmingham, were local rivals and the enemy of Birmingham City, their support containing a hooligan element nicknamed the 'C-Crew'. Tonight, the Zulus were looking for trouble, but they scored only a marginal success, with minor damage caused to the bar area of the pub and few casualties to brag about. Two young men were arrested.

The following day, Birmingham drew 0–0 with Villa at St Andrew's. After the match, disorder broke out again in various places on the route back to the city centre. Police on horseback tried to keep order but the eagerness of the opposing factions to engage in combat, and their apparent naked hatred for each other, made the task extremely difficult. Both groups chased through streets and in and out of traffic, with numerous bricks and similarly lethal projectiles being thrown by each side. Notable brawls took place in particular at Lancaster Circus, a large 'island' near the Central Fire Station, and along with the usual Zulu chants came frequent 'Shit on the Villa' songs too.

A fortnight later, on 21 September, Birmingham were at home to Leicester City and the routine was played out again: home groups circling the streets of the city centre, probing the policing at New Street Station and looking for away fans. The Zulu chant often sounded once again, now a battle cry for any number of youths, some of them perhaps not even connected to the gang. These hooligans might well have taken the film Zulu too much to heart but there was no disputing that their chanting possessed genuinely intimidating power.

On Saturday, 30 November, Blues played away at Arsenal in north London. Their supporters travelled in numbers, with a sizeable number of Zulus amongst them. The away fans were kept back for a period after the end of the football match and, as they pushed and jostled on the terraces, chants of 'Zulu' went up. In those days, 'Kill the Bill' was a familiar chant too, with certain members of society with a particularly strong dislike of the police having ACAB tattooed on their knuckles, standing for 'All Coppers Are Bastards'.

Chelsea, with their own notorious gang, the Headhunters, brought large numbers to Birmingham on Saturday, 21 December. After the game, police on horseback had to engage with rowdy Birmingham supporters and stones were thrown as they fought for control. Birmingham hooligans made for New Street to confront Chelsea fans and the usual chants went up while shoppers were jostled and pushed aside during the mêlée.

The following weekend, Birmingham City were at Manchester City, where the Zulu reputation had first been forged a few years before. A group of fifty youths chanting 'Zulu' confronted Manchester City supporters in the Arndale Centre before the game, fireworks were set off and fighting spilled over into some of the department stores.

Another away game, at Oxford United on 1 February 1986, saw a large number of Birmingham fans travel by train and by minibus. A group of around thirty Zulus made their presence felt with chanting and the usual efforts at avoiding being corralled by the police and the dog handlers with their German shepherds. Whilst Birmingham's hooligans now had a bad reputation around the country, many of the county police forces were not used to seeing such levels of organised violence. It wasn't unusual for away fans to be herded back to the railway station after the game even when some of them weren't even travelling by train, and stand-offs would occur as individuals berated the police, demanding they be allowed to go where they wanted to go. For any individuals who didn't want to pay a train fare it was a bonus because no ticket checks took place, but it was an unfortunate and too common example of normal supporters suffering unjustly, stained by the lousy reputation of the hooligans within their numbers. Back in Birmingham, football trains would often roll into Platform 12, the Parcels Yard, where people simply surged on to the platform and out through the gates in Station Street, opposite The Crown public house.

On Saturday, 8 February, Birmingham City were at home to West Bromwich Albion, one of the classic local derby games and very difficult to police, even with horses and motorcyclists deployed, owing to both sets of fans mingling in large numbers. Pre- and post-match skirmishes broke out at a number of places in and around Birmingham city centre and one twenty-four-year-old Albion fan suffered serious injuries when trying to escape a running street battle involving about fifty men in Digbeth. He was treated in the Major Injuries Unit at Birmingham Accident Hospital. 'At first it was thought that he had been struck with a hammer wielded by rival fans,' reported one newspaper. 'It later transpired that he had slipped on ice while attempting to flee and had struck his head violently on a lamp post.'

Another derby game followed the next Saturday when Blues were at near-neighbours Coventry City. This fixture always saw a lot of fans travel by train owing to the frequency of the services and shortness of the journey. This presented a strong test for the British Transport Police who, with limited resources, had to decide which trains to escort and which to let go unaccompanied. I sympathised with them. As a young BTP constable I had been part of one such escort bringing one of the Black Country teams into Coventry Station. There were three of us and the train was a three-car set with locked connecting doors in between. That meant each one of us having to man a crowded carriage alone, with no prospect of any help. I was in the middle carriage and stood at one end of it with my back against the locked door, facing the fans. En route, someone in one of the other coaches pulled the communication cord several times; each time, a huge cheer went up inside. Before reaching Coventry we went through a tunnel and someone switched the lights out, so that we were in complete darkness. I resisted the strong urge to pull my truncheon out because I knew that they would see it as a sign that I was worried. It wasn't worth it; even if scared it is better for an officer not to show emotion. When we finally reached our destination, I vented my adrenalin on one particularly vocal individual, leaving him in no doubt about where he would be heading if he didn't clear off quickly! Being a complete dickhead was not classified as a criminal offence, and I didn't have enough to arrest him, but he wasn't so brave when he was on his own. I sweated profusely that day but thankfully I coped.

The Coventry–Birmingham game was an 11.30 a.m. kick-off to reduce the amount of booze downed by supporters of either team and so people were on the move early that day. Official 'advice' on changing kick-off times came from our Football Hooliganism Guidance. This recommended that when a fixture was likely to attract a crowd well over the football ground's capacity or where public order problems might arise, then in consultation with the home club and the local police commander, one of the following alternatives must be agreed or otherwise implemented if the commander so directed: the match was to be all-ticket; it should be played at an alternative venue; or the day and time of the kick-off should be changed. In my opinion, early kick-offs make little difference to hooligans. The assumption that most of them misbehave because of drink was contradicted by our experience: whilst the older element were more hardened drinkers, the organised element of the Zulus were not. For many of them, the actual football game was an irrelevance, so it didn't matter what time it started. The same applied to those who used drugs. And, in effect, the hardened drinkers just got more down their necks in a shorter space of time.

A strong police presence kept the two sides apart that day but once again, as the ritual breakaway groups attempted to avoid the police, the Zulu chants went up.

March 15 saw four fans arrested for public order offences inside St Andrew's during the game with Tottenham Hotspur, and on 22 March, fighting occurred before, during and after yet another derby match, this time at Villa Park, where the pitch was invaded too. Police arrested more than seventy people in what the local press called 'one of the worst days of Midland soccer violence this season'. The police reported an atmosphere of 'extreme tension' during the game and the fighting spilled into the streets after the final whistle. More fights erupted at New Street Station when 800 fans left a train which had arrived from Witton. A policewoman was injured.

Seventeen fans were arrested for public order offences on 13 April, ten more on 24 April and another fourteen on 6 May. All three incidents occurred in John Bright Street, in the city centre, which was considered by the Zulu Warriors as their territory. They defended it strenuously against perceived opponents whilst resisting police efforts to control them. By now, the people of Birmingham were getting used to an almost weekly catalogue of reports of football-related mayhem. Events on the field had been almost equally abysmal, and saw City relegated along with their neighbours West Bromwich Albion.

With what had generally been a fateful season now over, an academic report on 28 May criticised English football in general, effectively accusing soccer clubs of failing to denounce racial hatred on the terraces a year after thirty-nine people had died at the Heysel Stadium in Brussels. The report, by the Independent Centre for Contemporary Studies, claimed football authorities had 'slept too soundly' on the build-up of racist and fascist groups at grounds in recent years. And on 17 June, it was reported that top police officers from throughout Britain were gathering in Birmingham to draw up new battle plans in the war on soccer thugs. New measures were being put together to make it more difficult for the hooligans who had 'driven families from the terraces'.

Events took an even more sinister turn that month when a car was overturned late at night outside the Custard House pub in Blake Lane, Stechford, by Zulu Warriors apparently living in the area. A similar incident had already happened outside The Mackadown pub a fortnight earlier, and on 29 June, The Broadway pub in Stechford was also hit. The motives for the criminal damage were not clear but protection/extortion and drugs-related turf disputes were thought to be distinctly possible.

On 30 June, the Birmingham Mail newspaper ran a headline report of a gang of youths who had boarded a bus and terrorised an elderly woman and two rival football fans. The youths, Blues fans and over thirty in number, chanted football slogans, threw seats through the windows of the bus, knocked the seventy-nine-year-old woman to the floor and chased two youths they believed to be rival football fans. Prosecutor James Orrel told Birmingham Crown Court that the youths were on a bus to the city centre from Erdington when two other youths who they believed to be Aston Villa fans also boarded the bus; scuffling soon broke out. The Villa fans got off the bus and tried to hide in the Norton Arms pub but were followed. Bricks and stones were thrown through the pub windows and one woman inside was slightly injured. The two youths left the pub in a car but were surrounded by the gang. Although they escaped again, the car was damaged. In court, seven youths admitted causing an affray, two of them were sent to youth custody and the others fined. One of them, just fifteen years of age and from the Bordesley Green area, was conditionally discharged; he would later become target number 12 in our police operation and was given the nickname of Orange. Judge Paul Clark was reported as saying, 'If this had been a colony of monkeys they would not have behaved as badly as these young men did,' which could easily have been construed as both ridiculous and inflammatory language.

In the summer of 1986 came more evidence of the Birmingham nightlife scene suffering overly aggressive times when a doorman was knocked to the ground, kicked, dragged into a toilet and bitten in the ear when he tried to stop a fight in a Birmingham club. The fight broke out in Boogies Brasserie in Lower Severn Street, after the manager asked the bouncer to get rid of some troublemakers. And on 20 July, police officers with riot helmets and shields had been called out to halt an attack by a gang of men on the Artful Dodger pub in Castle Vale. Robert Price, chairman of Birmingham licensing justices, said he would write to Home Secretary Douglas Hurd about the problem. The battle was said to be the latest in a catalogue of violence in and around city pubs. A report drawn up by the National Association of Licensed House Managers said nearly two hundred pub landlords in the Midlands had been victims of physical attacks in the previous year. 'We get more and more kids who do not hesitate to use violence,' said John Blunn, a Midland representative of NALHM. 'They throw glasses and bottles and use knives. I think they are treated too leniently by the courts where they are told not to be a naughty boy and do it again.' The release of the study was reported locally under the headline 'Landlords in Terror'. Although a definite link to the Zulus had yet to emerge, it seemed it would only be a matter of time.

*

The 1986–87 football season began in now familiar fashion with a free-for-all between two of the country's most active hooligan gangs, as the Sunday Mercury newspaper of 24 August reported:

> At Stoke-on-Trent, gangs of Birmingham City fans and Stoke City supporters clashed before and during the Division Two match at the Victoria Ground. Gangs of fans terrorised shoppers in the city centre shopping centre as they fought

with bricks and wooden staves before the game. More than 100 Birmingham fans arrived in Stoke in private cars and clashed with rival fans near the club's ground. Eight people were held inside the ground and later charged with Public Order offences. Another 16 were thrown out of the ground. Police said, 'We marshalled all the fans who arrived by train but were not aware of those who came to Stoke in private cars. By the time we got reinforcements to the scene of the fighting, the trouble had ended. There were also a number of skirmishes in the pubs on Saturday night involving fans of both teams.'

A month later, a large-scale fight broke out at the Mason Arms on the High Street, Solihull, just before pub closing time, after a match earlier that day at St Andrew's between Birmingham City and Ipswich Town. A doorman who tried to intervene was slashed in the face, apparently with a craft knife. Some of those involved gave out the telltale chant of 'Zulu!'

The use of knives in such confrontations would soon have terrible consequences. That October, a twenty-year-old Birmingham soccer fan, Quenton Belmont, and his West Ham-supporting friend were attacked by a gang of Millwall thugs on Villiers Street, London. Belmont was stabbed in the throat and chest. He managed to struggle free, bleeding heavily, before collapsing on the Thames Embankment, and was lucky to survive. His friend was not so fortunate: Terry Burns, aged nineteen, from Maidstone, Kent, died of chest wounds. The pair had been set upon in an unprovoked attack by up to a dozen drunken hooligans looking for rivals. It seemed that the tragic football fatalities of the previous year had had no effect on those bent on mayhem.

On 11 October, after Portsmouth beat the Blues 2–0 at Fratton Park, a group of twenty-five Zulu Warriors became isolated on a housing estate whilst purportedly trying to get back to their vehicles. They encountered a much larger group of the well-known 'Pompey' hooligan contingent the 6.57 Crew and a fierce fight ensued. Legend has it that in true military style the Zulus stood, formed a line and proceeded to win the battle decisively, despite the heavy odds against them. So was born the legend of the 'Portsmouth 25'. The Zulu Warriors were hugely proud of their brief history and would identify some fixtures for 'anniversary visits' in order to celebrate past achievements; the Portsmouth 25 fight was high on their list of battle honours. Triumphing against larger groups gave those who were there big kudos in the eyes of their peers. Newspaper reports later said that thirteen arrests were made during the fighting.

On 1 November, a police motorcyclist was temporarily blinded when fluid was sprayed in his face as he tackled a hundred-strong mob of football fans in West Bromwich town centre before the local derby with Birmingham City. The officer had moved in to disperse a crowd which had gathered at the junction of High Street and Bagnall Street. As he confronted chanting fans, a youth produced a black aerosol can and sprayed a substance into his face. The officer immediately felt a stinging sensation and was taken to Sandwell District General Hospital for treatment. Eighteen fans were arrested during the match.

Rival hooligan gang the Subway Army, supporters of

Wolverhampton Wanderers, left their own mark on the seaside resort of Torquay, Devon, that month. Two policemen were injured during violence before and during the Fourth Division game between home side Torquay United and Wolves. About fifty of the eight hundred travelling fans went on the rampage before the match. Several arrests were made and one officer was taken to hospital with a suspected fractured skull. The game was delayed in the second half for ten minutes after repeated pitch invasions.

Less seriously, indeed quite amusingly, another unrelated newspaper report appeared a few days later:

Police have increased security at their fortified crowd control box at Birmingham City's St Andrew's ground after a thief broke in. The box, which houses video cameras to catch hooligans on film, is specially fortified to withstand assaults from missiles and weapons. But a burglar stole radio equipment after breaking through boarding at the rear of the box. The thief took only equipment valued at about £100 but left behind thousands of pounds' worth of video equipment.

On the afternoon of 15 November, Birmingham City beat Millwall away 2–0. Millwall fans launched a planned attack after the match on the Zulus at London Bridge Station, with several neutral bystanders being injured too. This was a significant incident in hooligan history, as it may have been the first time any group confronted Millwall on their patch and actually bested them. A short while later, Liam, a constable in the West Midlands Police, was on match duty at West Bromwich

Albion, where Millwall were playing. Liam would later be deeply involved in Operation Red Card.

> LIAM: I locked up a bloke who was a big Millwall fan. I was having a chat with him in the custody block. He had a good job with Network Rail. I told him I was a Blues fan and he told me about an incident at London Bridge where they had arranged to meet the Zulus. He said, 'We got to the top of the bridge and all we heard was, Zulu, Zulu. It seemed like there was two hundred of them in a line. It was just a sea of black faces. I looked at my mate and said, "Shall we stand or shall we run?" We ran, and it was the first time I had ever seen Millwall run. It was like a scene from Zulu Dawn.'

The national media reported on 25 November that Prime Minister Mrs Thatcher planned to make football a members-only spectator sport the following season in a bid to curb hooliganism. 'The Government is ready to impose a member-ship card system on clubs if they do not agree to a voluntary scheme,' reported one newspaper. 'Card holders would be allowed to follow their teams to away games as well as supporting home games but no card would mean no entry. Talks between Ministers and the football authorities are still going on but so far the Football League is resisting such a proposal, they want a scheme with seventy per cent membership and the remainder for casual attendance. The Government has warned clubs that if they do not act it will legislate by adding new powers to the Safety In Sports Grounds bill it is introducing to the Commons next month.'

On 29 December, after a draw at St Andrew's, two Millwall supporters were seriously injured by Zulu Warriors outside New Street Station. The attack was committed predominantly by West Indian youths armed with a variety of weapons, and followed a Zulus Christmas party in the John Bright Street area of the city; it was clearly not the season of goodwill to all men. The popular pubs, clubs and bars in the area at that time included the Rumrunner, Boogies, Edwards No. 7 and 8, the Paramount, Millionaires, Kaleidoscope and The Crown. All witnessed depressingly frequent instances of violence and fighting.

In the early hours of New Year's Day, a man was seriously wounded in John Bright Street. We were to discover that the offender was a known associate of the Zulu gang. And late January brought a further indication of the gang's activities, although positive identifications were not possible at the time. 'Pick Axe Gang Attack Pub Man' was the headline in one local newspaper:

A man was seriously injured when a twenty-strong gang of hooded raiders wielding pick axe handles, hammers and baseball bats smashed up a Birmingham pub... Mr Brian Taylor was suffering from a suspected fractured skull after being beaten up in The Mountford pub, Kingshurst. Violence flared at 2 p.m. when the gang, wearing balaclava hats and scarves around their faces, burst into the bar. As terrified customers tried to escape, the gang began hitting out at anything... Mr Taylor, who is in his late 20s and lives in School Close, Kingshurst, was drinking with friends at the time. He was recovering at

East Birmingham Hospital where his condition was said to be quite comfortable. Other customers were injured, including Mr Stephen Goodard aged 32 years of Mackadown Lane, Tile Cross who suffered a broken arm, and Mr Alan Lingard of Stockfield Road, Acocks Green who received an arm injury. Police believed the gang may have been looking for somebody but did not know the motive for the attack. After the five-minute wrecking spree the men made off in cars at high speed. An Incident Room has been set up at Chelmsley Wood Police Station and witnesses urged to come forward.

The attackers had links to the Zulu Warriors and were said here to be supporting the activities of a Birmingham drugs dealer. There were similar suspicions concerning attacks in the pubs the Tilt Hammer and The Rainbow.

Then came the tipping point.

*

Harry Doyle was a strapping police officer: tall, well built and quite capable of looking after himself in a tight spot. But when the twenty-five-year-old constable entered a Birmingham nightclub called Boogies, at around 11 p.m. on Saturday, 10 January 1987, he was off-duty, alone, and venturing into hostile territory. Boogies, a three-tiered city centre venue, was popular with known Zulu Warriors. The premises were full, the norm for a Saturday night, with plenty of men celebrating Birmingham City's 1–0 win at Ipswich Town in the FA Cup third round. Doyle's short haircut and smart, clean-cut appearance ensured he caught the attention of a few undesirables. Why he was there, alone or not – why he even entered that notorious Zulu haunt – was never fully explained. The fact is he should not have been anywhere near the place.

It was fairly normal in those times for off-duty officers to use their police warrant cards to gain access to clubs and the like, thus avoiding paying entrance fees. Club owners generally welcomed their presence but the character of some of the Boogies door staff, employed for how well they could handle themselves rather than their respect, if there was any, for the police, could well have contributed towards what happened next. Certain people in the club that night may even have suspected Doyle was working in an undercover role. He was not; he was simply out on the town for a drink.

He certainly paid for his mistake. What happened was recounted in the book Zulus, by author Caroline Gall: 'As everyone knew each other in the bar, a large, well-built stranger walking in and proceeding to drink alone was immediately noticed and aroused suspicion. Some of the lads engaged in a bit of conversation with him and discovered he'd had a bit to drink, as he told them to shut up with their Zulu nonsense because they didn't realise who he was and they couldn't touch him, or words to that effect.' Whatever the warped reasons for the ensuing attack were, Doyle was punched and knocked to the floor, and a broken glass was thrust into his face. His wounds required thirty-two stitches.

A police spokesman subsequently told reporters: 'PC Doyle struggled to his feet and then one man picked up a glass and thrust it into his face, inflicting severe cuts on the left side. It was an unprovoked attack.' He said Doyle, a plain-clothes officer based at Digbeth Police Station, was attacked because he was recognised as being a policeman. He was treated at Birmingham Accident Hospital. 'The man who used the glass was described as white, aged about twenty-two, with blond, collar length hair parted in the centre,' added the police spokesman.

The police launched an investigation for the offence of wounding with intent to cause grievous bodily harm, commonly known as a Section 18, or 'GBH'. Three people were subsequently arrested. Two of them were considered prominent in the Zulu hierarchy and one later received a substantial prison sentence for the attack. We would learn that two of our eventual Red Card targets were present in Boogies at the time of the savage beating, though they were not directly involved in it; they would be named 'Specs' and 'Sheet'. Specs would be target number 45 and Sheet, who wore a three-quarter-length white jacket, target number 75.

The attack received extensive media coverage and dramatic photographs of Doyle's injuries, consisting of horrific cuts to his left eye, which was swollen closed as a result, down and across to his upper lip, made the newspapers. It was headline material that none of us ever wanted to see, but it did serve as a catalyst for good. The Zulu Warriors had finally gone too far. It was time for something to be done.

Adam, who would be a part of our operation, knew PC Doyle.

ADAM: I saw Harry Doyle after he had been attacked in Boogies. His face was a hell of a mess. I knew him as he drank in a pub called the Adam & Eve. I spoke to him about what happened and he said something like he had seen someone he knew and next thing he got glassed. We heard that the senior officers had been to the club and made it known that this had got to be sorted out and that whoever had done it needed to come forward. I remember that when we were doing our background enquiries it was clear that Francis [target number 1] knew the people who had been involved.

Some might say the police were slow to respond to the threat posed by the Zulus. I would disagree. In 1986, crime pattern analysis and the linking of offences and offenders was not so evident, except in major crime cases such as a serial murderer. Here we had a group who were shoplifting in Birmingham and elsewhere in the UK, but with each police force investigating crimes committed in their own areas. Some of 'our' hooligan group were also involved in smashing up pubs and terrorising the licensees on the E Division and the F Division of Birmingham but with little actual tie between the two. Some of those individuals went to football games but were not attached to the Zulu gang, while some unquestionably were; some were burglars and thieves. None of these matters could easily be linked together and no one fully understood the extent of the gang's criminal activities. If ever any were arrested for a public order offence, they were dealt with for that particular offence, and that was it.

 Harry Doyle was not a friend of mine but he was a fellow

officer and that was enough for me to say that we had to do our best to find out who had attacked him. I did not feel anything personally in relation to the attack. In my experience, getting personal blurs your ability to focus on doing a good job. Emotions were best kept out of it. The attack on Harry Doyle was regarded as an attack on the police service as a whole. It could not be tolerated or allowed to go unpunished; it had to be placed at the top of our priorities list. It was already a long list, of course. Once people lose their fear of attacking the police then you have anarchy and everybody suffers. This could not be allowed to happen. The thin blue line was just that and it had to be protected. We possibly should have responded earlier, but a pertinent question would be, responded to what, exactly? There were so many different offences taking place that crime solving and prevention was like an overcrowded minefield, and only when we had a full-time team dedicated to the gang were we able to link the various strands of data together.

Following the attack, senior officers from the F Division of West Midlands Police, which covers Birmingham city centre, expressed deep concerns about the activities of the Zulu Warriors. Pub licensees were complaining of intimidation by them and it was strongly suspected that many of the group were engaged in organised criminality, ranging from serious public order offences to large-scale shoplifting expeditions around the country. The divisional chief superintendent directed that the Zulus' activities be explored and that a strategy be devised to combat them. The seed of Operation Red Card was sown.

CHAPTER 4

GENESIS

T HE INITIAL TASK of looking at what we knew about the Zulus and studying the feasibility of mounting some kind of operation against them came to rest on me. I was already involved in another big investigation called Operation Century, which was due to run for another month or so, so I would need to free some time for this new project. But I was immediately attracted to the idea of doing something different – an operation into a major football gang – and to be the first in West Midlands Police to do it. It certainly looked like a challenge. At thirty-four years of age, I was relatively young but already an experienced detective sergeant. I was ready.

I am not ashamed to admit I was also personally ambitious. From April 1985, I had spent short secondments with the Force Surveillance Unit, the CID at Bradford Street Police Station and the Shoplifting Squad at Steelhouse Lane, before taking on the new post there of detective sergeant (local intelligence officer) in August 1986. I had also qualified for promotion to inspector level and, like a number of others in a similar position, been put into post to make a positive difference. There was no doubt that we were being judged and our personal advancement would be based on our results. I loved the responsibility, the decision-making and the managing of staff that all came with being a detective, and having got on to the first rung of the ladder I wanted to climb higher. And personally, although I had no interest in football or any other sport aside from perhaps snooker, I hated violence and despised those who inflicted it on others just because they could. I relished the task ahead.

Operation Century was co-ordinated by me and ran for most of March 1987. It resulted in the arrest of eighty-four people for vehicle crime on the F Division. Our tactics involved the use of the Divisional Observations Teams, known as DOTs, who were specially selected to keep watch from old 'bangers' and second-hand vans. The DOTs were formed at the time I took up the role of detective sergeant (local intelligence officer) and it was natural that we would come to use them for our future anti-Zulu operation, although their sergeant was always quick to remind me, 'Don't forget these are my staff, not yours. You don't get to do what you like with them all the time.'

The previous year, I had been given a relatively new role in local intelligence to, in police jargon, enhance our ability to respond proactively. This meant tactically or strategically getting ahead of the opposition. We wanted to know what they were going to do before they did it, and to stop them if we could. The police are a twenty-four-hour, seven days a week organisation, and the bulk of personnel are constables. As a probationer constable, I was issued with a little yellow booklet on my arrival at the training centre, entitled Useful

Definitions for Police Officers. It began with the words: 'A Constable is a citizen locally appointed under the Crown for the protection of life and property, the maintenance of order, the prevention and detection of crime, and the prosecution of offenders against the peace.'

'Response' policing is just that: waiting for the crime or incident to happen and then investigating it, whereas being proactive means digging deeper to identify crime patterns, trends and methods. It involves writing Sequence of Events charts and spotting links between individuals, groups and associates, gathering intelligence and grading it to establish its worth. My role as a local intelligence officer was to implement what we called the Intelligence Cycle: direction, collection, evaluation, analysis, dissemination. I had then to apply the right tactics to tackle each specific problem, whether that involved the use of covert methods, informants, or disruption.

In addition to the intelligence staff, I also tasked the DOT, who were trained in static and foot surveillance. I had spent three months on the Force Surveillance Unit in 1985 and failed miserably to read maps upside down whilst haring along in fast cars but it gave me a good grounding in the principles of effective surveillance. All of this I would apply to what became Operation Red Card. The idea was to get so close to the gang and to monitor them so astutely that we even learned what they had for breakfast.

There is a marked difference between being a uniformed police officer and a detective in the CID. The police uniform is a visible symbol of authority and very few members of the public look beyond the uniform at the person wearing it. You can have ten minutes or ten years in uniform, it doesn't matter in terms of people's perceptions. A plain-clothes CID officer has no such visible symbol of authority and therefore has to rely more on personality and style to create a presence. It is complex. The criminal community see the CID as something to worry more about if they are arrested. Uniformed officers generally worked fixed shifts and were usually able to go home on time when their set shift time had ended. CID officers however, generally worked long hours and therefore played harder socially too.

There is no doubt that during the course of my CID career between 1976 and 1988, my family came a clear second. I routinely worked ten hours a day, often twelve hours, and fifteen hours or more was not uncommon. The frequently asked question 'When are you coming home?' was met with the equally frequent reply 'When I am ready.' Whilst I supported my family financially, the reality is that I was absent for much of the time and I missed much of my children's growing up. Most of us were the same in those days; it was our way of life and no apologies were made. All that said, a good CID officer never lost sight of his roots. We all started the same as a PC on the beat so trying to play the hotshot detective would never work with colleagues or be tolerated.

My chief super, Clive Roche, proved to be a great supporter as things developed and without his backing I would not have been able to take matters further. In those days, a mere detective sergeant would see his chief superintendent formally perhaps once a year for a personal career review, but as events unfolded I was fortunate enough to have routine access to him if I felt I needed it. I would go on to have various key meetings with him to monitor the progress of the operation but this level of access did not always go down well with my immediate supervisors, who were used to a more orthodox, hierarchical approach. I was not particularly concerned about that. I was interested only in getting the job done and done well.

As well as the chief superintendent, as a CID officer I still came under the overall line management of the divisional detective superintendent, Roy Taylor, an immensely experienced individual with a full head of silver-grey hair. He was both a thoughtful, methodical worker and not known for taking great risks. My proposals were both risky and also a potential drain on his finite resources, so I had a lot of convincing to do. It was soon established that whilst we had a good deal of information on the gang, it was too fragmented and often not sufficiently up to date. In the early days of my feasibility study, Roy would often look at me from behind his desk, over the top of his glasses, and say, 'I think you need to develop this a bit further, Mike.' This was a sort of code for, 'Go away, I don't think you've got enough.' That said, I believe that he trusted me and accepted my later reassurances that everything would be okay. It was a tricky situation but I could not afford to make an enemy of him. Even at this stage, the Zulu Warriors were not a clearly defined group. Although they were a presence in the early 1980s, their origins were unclear to us. They had, however, unquestionably come to the fore by the time of the 'Leeds Riot' at Birmingham City in May 1985.

Whilst the Zulu Warriors retained their affinity to Birmingham City, it could be argued that their interest in the actual game of football had diminished considerably by 1987. Fewer of the hardcore regularly attended matches, no doubt partly due to the installation of CCTV in grounds and because they knew that their anonymity was no longer guaranteed. Francis, our lead target, was a prime example: he regularly attacked rivals in the name of football yet our observations showed he actually attended very few games. I believed their allegiance to the club merely supplied the focus on which to base their criminal activities. Smoking cannabis was also the order of the day for many of them (hard drugs were much less common in Birmingham then) while some of the older ones enjoyed plenty of booze. But the reality is that many of the Zulus were driven by the thrill and the adrenalin rush of a mass brawl.

The group had no known political affiliations. They did not usually wear identifying clothing other than the street fashion of the day, and whilst many had previous criminal convictions, a large number of them were seemingly 'normal', whatever the definition of what normal was, and in full-time jobs. Many came from the Stechford and Bordesley Green areas, covered by the E Division of West Midlands Police, and had known each other from school days, so there were very strong bonds within their ranks.

Whilst there was no indisputable direct link to the Zulu Warriors yet, a report in the Birmingham Evening Mail that

January, which made mention of the Operational Support Unit, detailed the lengths to which the police were now having to go to stop fighting between rival factions:

Riot Police equipped with helmets and full length shields were on standby for this afternoon's big FA cup soccer clash between Walsall and Birmingham City at Fellows Park. They were part of a massive operation by West Midlands Police to prevent fighting between rival fans. Three to four times the normal number of police were on duty at the ground and in key parts of the ground. For the first time, mounted police patrolled the town centre. Back-up units from the West Midlands Police Operational Support Unit equipped with riot gear were also on standby. Also present were officers based around St Andrew's who knew the Birmingham City troublemakers... In the main, trouble was curtailed and a group of 150 Birmingham fans making for Walsall town centre were rounded up and put back on trains for Birmingham and a 'potential bloodbath avoided'.

In fact it was later confirmed that police had made 43 arrests after Walsall dumped City out of the cup, as a subsequent report noted:

The game was held up briefly after half time when one man ran onto the pitch. He was tackled by police officers and marched away. Only minutes earlier officers drove a wedge between chanting Blues and Walsall supporters. Police swooped on the troublemakers and five mounted policemen in riot gear raced on to the pitch to avert further incidents. Officers from the Operational Support Unit were on duty at the Railway End. At the opposite end of the ground a fight broke out. Birmingham City fans had got into the Walsall section. Officers were running from all points towards the fighting along with mounted police. Police officers went into the crowd to prevent an invasion but the excitement stepped up by the fighting at the opposite end made things worse.

Press reports also appeared about Birmingham traders being hit by a gang of organised shoplifters calling themselves the Zulus. The shopkeepers said that they were losing hundreds of pounds' worth of goods a week to the gang, who entered stores in large groups, terrorised staff and effectively looted the place. The proprietor of Cheap Jeans, a clothing store in Corporation Square in the city, said the gang were stealing their stock on a daily basis. 'Groups of between eight and twelve of them come into the shop and tell my three staff that the Zulus will get them if they resist,' said the owner, Jay Chouhan. 'They normally all carry large sports bags which they stuff with clothes and leather jackets.' He said another shop nearby had recently been stripped of forty pairs of trousers and thirty shirts in a single raid.

Another newspaper report highlighted the new tactic of 'steaming' employed by shoplifters:

Police and traders throughout the Midlands have been hit hard by a new type of shop theft involving organised packs of young thieves... Hundreds of thousands of pounds' worth of stock is being lost to gangs who enter shops in large numbers to

*intimidate staff... Police define 'steaming' as a mass invasion
of a shop by a group of between six and twenty people in which
an implied threat is used. In Birmingham, where steaming
has become a problem in a number of larger shopping thoroughfares, police are joining forces with the city centre Traders
Anti-Theft Group in a drive to stamp out the problem. Inspector
Alan Seager, head of the city centre Shoplifting Squad, said the
shops most at risk were clothing stores.*

We believed, in fact we knew, that there was a link between
these steaming gangs and the Zulus – which was all the more
reason for us to target them.

*

While we had to wait and hope for permission from our bosses
to commence a targeted operation, we could at least begin
preliminary observations. On 7 February 1987, I and a number
of staff from a divisional obs team did our first recce at New
Street Station. Two of the DOT, Don and Reece, would work
undercover and out of uniform. Both were relatively young in
service but committed officers who knew their street craft.
The railway station had a number of black-and-white cameras
so we were able to monitor most of the activity remotely in
British Rail's CCTV control room in the station. The cameras
were operated by rail employees rather than police.

Birmingham City were playing away that day at Derby
County. Just after 9 a.m., small groups of men and youths
started to gather on the station concourse, including two

who for some unknown reason were wearing French Foreign Legion caps. Prominent in one group was a black guy sporting a brown deerstalker hat and a plain scarf wrapped around his face. They obviously had their own views on headgear but to my mind there was not much fashion sense amongst the Zulu Warriors. Among them were also some of what I referred to as the 'B Team'.

The supporters travelling by train to the Derby match, including the hooligan element, were accompanied by a small number of BTP officers. One group of about sixty fans left the train early at Burton-upon-Trent to meet others already there. This tactic, of alighting early at stops en route rather than the final destination, challenged officers to keep pace with the various groups' movements. At the same time, unsuspecting landlords in areas along the route would suddenly find their pub full of packs of rather lively young men. With limited resources, the BTP always faced the dilemma of whether or not to get off the train with the departing group in these circumstances or to stay on with the remaining fans. Quick decisions were needed in what were effectively no-win situations for which someone nevertheless would be held accountable.

A little later that day, a known shoplifter and Zulu Warrior, 'Stan', was seen on New Street Station, as well as a tall black male accompanied closely by a white friend, who moved from group to group engaging them in conversation. No doubt their planning was under way. Over four hundred in all travelled by train to Derby. Derby Station had an enclosed bridge connecting the platforms, with access to the front and back of the station too. A chanting crowd in such a space made a huge noise because it was enclosed, adding to the intimidating atmosphere and the sense of drama. The norm was for visiting fans to be corralled by the local police and escorted to the football ground via the train station's rear access area. The home fans knew this, however, and so there was always potential for an ambush.

County's thug followers, the so-called Derby Lunatic Fringe, had quite a bad reputation too. However, we saw no trouble that day. At least our limited observations confirmed the strong presence of Zulu Warriors and their police-dodging tactics. We had made a start. We had also grabbed some good still photographs in Birmingham city centre of individuals outside The Crown pub at midday, some of whom were establishing themselves as main targets of our operation, such as 'Checkers', who became target number 13. We achieved this by getting access to a first floor office in a building opposite the pub. This static observation point would prove to be very important.

Although we were still operating only at a provisional level at this stage, our undercover officers would be part of a multi-faceted team rather than having the burden of everything standing or falling on them. I also proposed that we operated under Major Incident Room guidelines, and although computers were considered, we finally decided on using manual indexes instead. I wanted to keep the operation as tight as possible, and using computers would have involved more staff and more cost. At that point I had no idea how many targets we would come up with; if I had known, I would have opted to use them. I had to make a decision but hindsight in policing has proved to be a frail excuse! Pending the outcome of discussions at a very senior level, it was agreed to take preliminary action, even though we were already well into the 1986–87 football season. At that stage I named the operation 'Rourke's Drift' after the famous battle in the Anglo–Zulu War, not realising I had misspelled the name – it should be Rorke's.

Birmingham City played Brighton & Hove Albion the following Saturday, 14 February. We made video tape recordings of sections of the crowd at the game and again took still photographs outside The Crown. While we did not fully know it at the time, we were fishing in the right ponds. All the still photographs were date- and time-stamped and generally black and white, providing excellent evidence of association, clothing worn and identification. A target we nicknamed 'Light' was noted as being there and would be added to our list as number 24.

To help with my feasibility study into an anti-Zulus operation, I contacted a relatively new department known as TO20 within the Metropolitan Police in London. They dealt with public order. I spoke to several of their experts who were the architects of a landmark operation called Own Goal, aimed at halting escalating football hooliganism in the London area. On 18 February, about six weeks after the attack on Harry Doyle and a week or so after we had started our preliminary observations, I went to a detailed debrief in the capital with the operations chief inspector from my division, Ian Garrett, who I got on with well. Short and unassuming, he had a propensity to talk quickly at times, but he was always smiling and positive, which suited me fine. We met some of the TO20 officers and were able to get a very detailed picture of past and present operations into hooligan factions linked to West Ham United, Millwall, Chelsea and Arsenal. We also met two officers from Leeds who had undertaken a covert operation against organised football violence in their area, and a DCI from the Force Intelligence Bureau updated me on their operation: they had four undercover officers working full time on the job, a sergeant and three constables. Each of them worked away from police premises in independent offices so as to preserve their false identities.

A Metropolitan Police commander started the briefing. During the introduction, another senior officer stressed that considerable interest and support had come from the Home Office and from the Football Association, so serious was the problem. Reservations had initially been expressed from high up about mounting such operations due to the manpower and overtime costs involved. It became widely accepted however that undercover operations were necessary and that removing prime hooligan targets was actually a cost-effective way of reducing police cover at previous trouble spots. The fact that none of their officers working covertly had been identified by gang members as police officers, despite some of them achieving a high level of penetration of the gangs, was recognised as a mark of their skill, courage and fortitude. Media coverage of such arrests sent out a very positive message to the public too, which it was felt should not be underestimated. Having the general public on your side is always a bonus.

We explained to the Met that we were on a fact-finding mission with a view to mounting a similar operation in our own area. We also managed to spend a couple of very useful hours with some of their undercover officers. This all felt like excellent preparation for our plans in Birmingham. In the main meeting, updates were provided on the Met operations. In the West Ham United case, twelve targets were arrested and various weapons and incriminating photographs were recovered. Some initial targets from West Ham's notorious Inter City Firm had been identified from a BBC Television documentary about them and from an academic book called Hooligans Abroad. In the Millwall operation, eighteen main targets were arrested, with stolen property, weapons and newspaper cuttings recovered. Significant intelligence about a murder investigation was also gained. In the Chelsea operation, Own Goal, an update was given about an ongoing trial which included conspiracy evidence going back over four years and involving another group of supporters linked to violence in Paris as they travelled to Madrid, where England were due to play Spain.

Coincidentally, media reports emerged of Birmingham followers' involvement with trouble surrounding the same England game – ironically classified as a friendly – in Madrid, which England won 4–2:

Twenty-two soccer hooligans, many of them from the West Midlands, have been arrested in France and Spain after running clashes with the authorities which again brought shame to British football. In Spain, 12 thugs including fans from Tipton and Warley, beat up a ticket collector and attempted to throw him off the train taking a party of British soccer supporters to the England match in Madrid. They also attacked other passengers, molested women on the train and caused damage as they hurled beer cans around the carriages. In another incident, Spanish police arrested six fans who ran amok in the northern town of Burgos. In France, a cafe owner in the red light district of Paris was attacked and beaten up after a group of four fans wearing National Front regalia tried to leave without paying for drinks. The four were among a party of ten, some from Birmingham, who were detained following a series of fights.

In the Arsenal operation, twelve people were targeted and a serious affray in Deptford, south London, was cleared up. And in the Leeds operation, called Wild Boar, some seventy hardcore targets had been infiltrated, of which around a dozen were due to be arrested. Some were believed to be involved in other criminality. That operation had encountered some opposition from senior officers, mainly because they feared for the safety for the undercover officers involved.

I learned more about the subculture of football hooligans and their methods as well as such things as gangs' usage of calling cards and the like: 'Millwall Bushwackers – we will be waiting for you down at the Den. We are evil.' Chelsea's mob had cards saying, 'You have been nominated and dealt with by the Chelsea Headhunters.' Arsenal's had 'The Gooners AFC Hooligan Firm' with a skull and crossbones design. West Ham's Inter City Firm often left victims with cards declaring,

'You have been visited by the Inter City Firm', while Leeds United hooligans used, 'With compliments Leeds United VYT' (their so-called Very Young Team), with a picture of a crown and the words 'By appointment to Her Majesty the Queen' and 'Danger: Government Health Warning, Leeds Fans Can Seriously Damage Your Health.' We knew the Zulu Warriors came up with their own versions, some of which were adhesive peel-offs which they stuck on the clothing of their battered victims. For me this was where some of those supposedly normal people became abnormal in their behaviour.

I was gradually gathering support within my divisional management for the concept of mounting a similar operation to those carried out by other forces. This internal backing was critical, as it was clear to me that I would need certain CID colleagues to contribute. Some of them still felt that mucking around with football crowds was not proper detective work, so the help rendered by the Metropolitan Police and by the officers from Leeds was invaluable. However, I was clear in my mind I would do it my own way. There were aspects of their operations which I felt could be improved or changed (and, without conceit or arrogance, I believe that subsequent court outcomes proved me right). I decided that we would make as much use of technical equipment as we could, bearing in mind the need to comply with the law and proportionality, the need to show that crimes being investigated are serious enough to warrant the use of technical equipment and intrusive covert tactics. I knew that while the evidence of undercover officers would be crucial, it would carry even more weight if supported by good video and photographs.

Chief Inspector Garrett produced an advice document laying out the terms of reference for the team's infiltration of targets. 'At matches, very close and direct association with targets may force an officer to become more involved in charges or attacks on other groups of supporters than is clearly desirable,' it said. 'We are there to observe possible offences and must be careful how far we ourselves go or become involved in such incidents. When violence and serious disorder takes place it may lay officers open to allegations at court that they acted as hooligans themselves, by their very active participation or aiding and abetting the build up to the events i.e. "Agent Provocateur", a grey and dangerous area. Operationally there are few benefits and many pitfalls from over infiltration of targets, in engaging in activities beyond the close and careful surveillance and observation of suspects which falls just short of close and direct association.'

*

The weekend after I had picked the brains of the Metropolitan Police teams, Blues played away at Ipswich Town and we had our first trip out. It was an uneventful day but we managed to photograph a target group and obtained tapes of the CCTV footage at the Portman Road ground, which clearly showed some of the B Team hooligans trying to goad opposition fans by beckoning them to fight. These B Team characters hardly looked old enough to shave. They were not being that brave either, owing to the enormous fence separating the two groups on the terraces. In my opinion they were trying to live out their fantasies; my concern was that at some point they would turn those fantasies into reality as their confidence developed. Equally depressing, for me, was the sight of a line of police officers standing against the fence on the Birmingham supporters' side; they were within easy reach of these hooligans yet did nothing, instead remaining still with their arms folded and with fixed stares. It wasn't the first or last time I saw such passive behaviour, which served only to embolden the hooligans and put the police in a bad light. It was unacceptable. Some of my colleagues used to refer to it as the 'cardboard cut-out syndrome' and it wasn't meant as a compliment.

Watching this episode on camera, I did not once see any of the group turn their attention towards events on the football pitch, despite the fact that the game still had more than twenty minutes to go.

We continued to obtain video evidence of association, and still photography, at different locations such as New Street Station, The Crown, the St Andrew's ground and the nearby Watering Hole pub, all known haunts of our targets. We also went to more away games and started to develop cover stories and safety procedures. At the same time, we started a manual card index to draw all of the intelligence together, including records of ejections from stadiums and arrests made at home and away fixtures for the current and the previous season. A small vehicle index and photo index was also established. On the day of observations there would be me and three officers from the DOT. I liaised with the British Transport Police too to keep up to speed with supporter numbers travelling and we would have at least one officer in the Network Rail control room to make a contemporaneous written incident log sheet of relevant events he saw on CCTV. Two other officers would spend some time wandering around New Street Station, outside The Crown and in the city centre, on fact-finding and familiarisation exercises.

At the time, St Andrew's bore the marks of both pro- and anti-Zulu graffiti on the walls next to the stiles, including swastika and National Front insignia. The obscenities and general malice gave some example of the grim atmosphere pervading the place, although almost as depressing was the fact that no one at the club had seen fit to remove the graffiti, which added to the bleak nature of the exterior.

We are back
Zulus are Wogs
Zulus are Muggers
Keep Britain White BCFC
Zulu Fuck Off AVFC

Our initial observations lasted for five weeks. Some of the best evidence we gathered was against a number of the B Team involved in an incident at St Andrew's on 28 February. Earlier that week, I had been to the ground when it was empty to liaise with a local inspector and to familiarise myself with the stadium layout. The Kop terrace was split into two, with a capacity for 5,000 home supporters in what was called the Home Match Day Casual side and for slightly more in the Home Members section. The Spion Kop was Birmingham City territory and any visiting fans foolhardy enough to enter there would do so at their peril. The total capacity of St Andrew's was 25,728 which included space for nearly 7,000 visiting fans.

As with most football clubs it was not an easy environment to police, especially if the order of the day for many followers was disorder. The vast majority of officers policing the match were just drafted in on a Saturday and for many of them it was seen as either an opportunity to watch the match or a chore to be completed with the minimum of fuss and as quickly as possible. They did not want to be there and knew that if they arrested anyone they would very possibly end up rolling around on the floor with the suspect and then be late to finish work because of all the consequent paperwork. I have known senior officers to openly discourage arrests because it would diminish their deployable resources. There was some overtime for football and the BTP in particular would be on twelve-hour shifts to compensate for the fact that they had to provide travelling serials of officers, hence 6 a.m. to 6 p.m. and 6 p.m. to 6 a.m. for instance so that the afternoon shift could travel over in the afternoon to bring away fans back. In my experience, few police officers wanted to cover football matches and those that did eventually got fed up even with the overtime, as ultimately it was not much recompense or a great comfort. Job satisfaction is on the whole more important than bonuses in pay.

The match on that day was Birmingham City against Hull City, and as the game went on the police had to eject a misbehaving youth from the Kop, during the course of which a sergeant was attacked and suffered a bruised face. I had covert officers Don and Reece in the Spion Kop, while I was in the police control room with access to the CCTV screens. By choice, Don and Reece have not contributed any personal recollections for this book, but I had great faith in them and tremendous admiration and respect for their contributions, and their actions speak for themselves. We learned much later that two friends of the B Team were ejected after a mêlée in the first half of the game, and at half time one of our covert officers in the crowd heard two B Teamers say that in the second half they were 'going to run the Bill' to create a 'come on' situation. Our coverts could not get any information to us at the time without breaking their cover, so they just had to pray that events did not get too volatile.

The crowd was raucous throughout the afternoon and some of them certainly were intent on enticing a police officer into the throng, with a view to attacking him. They aimed to do this by staging a mock fight, causing a large gap to open up in the crowd. Four white men started pushing and pulling each other, then a black youth ran across the terraces seemingly chased by three more white men who, one after the other, pretended to attack him by running and jumping up at him and then retreating, clapping, as if they had 'won' something. A gap opened immediately in front of a safety barrier; it was at least fifteen feet wide and ten feet deep. I was alarmed at the sight of a police inspector naively falling for the ruse and entering that gap alone. But despite various yobs waving others on and trying to encourage them to close in on the officer behind his back, no one actually had the courage to make the first move, thankfully. The inspector was eventually joined by a serial of officers who stood their ground among the crowd until more colleagues arrived to help quell the situation. It could have been grave and the inspector was very fortunate.

On the plus side, we had covert and video evidence of the incident and subsequently five of the B Team faced an indictment for unlawful assembly. It was pure luck that the charges were not much more severe. As we progressed in our work, we also compiled a numbered list of targets from the gang. Because we were not aware of the real names of many of them, nicknames were invented. Some of these were self-explanatory, some more random. Involved in the mock fight and potentially serious trap were 'Sharp', 'Benetton', 'Dek', 'Grace' and 'Baseball Cap'.

On Tuesday, 3 March, we headed off to a night game at Huddersfield Town's Leeds Road ground, not the most attractive venue (one end was fittingly called the Cowshed). It was not very productive in terms of evidence either, but we were honing our skills and the long journey home in the dark gave us plenty of time to discuss future tactics. On Saturday, 14 March, we attended another away game, at Crystal Palace in London, the home of the 'Selhurst Scalpers CPFC'. Again we were able to gather video material from New Street Station as well as from the Metropolitan Police, which included some Hoolivan footage. Used at high-profile matches, the Hoolivan was a new weapon in the fight against hooliganism: a hi-tech police van with protective grilles that enabled officers to maintain radio contact with officers inside and outside the ground and to video events outside.

The following Saturday we covered Birmingham's home game with Portsmouth and got more good evidence against the core group of Zulus. And on 28 March I went with officers to Barnsley in South Yorkshire, having liaised with their chief superintendent the week before, for the away game there. It was fairly uneventful but we were becoming known nationally and were generally welcomed by the other police forces; they knew the reputation of the Zulus and so any assistance was gratefully acknowledged.

ADAM: Mike [Layton] took us up in his car so there was a bit of ducking down beneath the seats when we got closer to the ground. He dropped us off and we were feeling uneasy. We had both worked in uniform all over the place and were worried about bumping into people who would recognise us and Colin was a born and bred Brummie. As it was it was a quiet day but it gave us a chance to settle into the job. Because of the 'blagging culture' on the OSU we used to try to avoid them when we were out. One day an officer actually called to us on the streets. It was a stupid thing to do and put us at risk.

COLIN: The first game I went to was at Barnsley. I went up in the car with Mike and Adam. Nothing happened but it was a weird feeling. When we got there I felt totally exposed. It was strange to be amongst these people having been in uniform only days before. I felt very vulnerable although it was reassuring to have the two spotters around (Mark and Liam). We met back at Barnsley Police Station after the game and had a couple of drinks in the police social club before travelling home. Not the sort of thing that you would do now but you didn't have risk assessments in those days.

A few days before the Barnsley journey, an interview with Assistant Chief Constable Paul Leopold appeared in the local press. Headlined 'Thug Buster', the feature allowed the fifty-one-year-old Londoner to disclose his thoughts and intentions regarding football hooliganism in our area:

In his Lloyd House, seventh floor city centre office, Leopold reveals details of a vastly expensive war that sounds as if it were aimed at an organisation of master criminals rather than bunches of trouble-for-kicks crowd stirrers. 'We have built up a huge intelligence system,' he says. 'Football Intelligence Officers pass up-to-the-minute information and pictures of troublemakers to the police forces all over the country.' He went on, 'Some Forces have gone undercover – casually dressed, unrecognisable policemen winning the confidence of near-psychopathic ringleaders and their tribe before arresting them at dead of night, as they have with Chelsea and West Ham followers. At the moment there is no particular reason why we should follow this practice but things could change. We have learned a great deal from recent breakdowns in public order. Closed circuit TV has had a major impact. There have been a large number of arrests after the cameras have recorded the faces of troublemakers. You can see just who they are. They don't watch the football at all. Often they even have their backs to the play, searching for possible causes to stir up. The thug leader actually tries to generate disorder by gesticulation, encouragement of violence and mocking behaviour. Drink contributes and it seems contradictory to me that fans can be stopped from drinking on coaches and outside the ground and yet can buy alcohol inside the grounds. I also believe blatant foul play on the field, dissension or obvious disagreement with a referee's decision may spark violence on the terraces if fans are inclined that way.'

If they are, here is Leopold's identikit of a hooligan leader: He will be in his late teens or early twenties, male and physically fit and from any part of the country. He can 'run fast and punch hard'. From a wide spectrum of social groups, from unemployed to teacher or solicitor, more likely than not to have a criminal record which is unconnected to football. He carries some sort of weapon. ACC Leopold said, 'Finding hammers or iron bars is nothing unusual. Taped between the cheeks of the backside is one favourite place for concealment of such weapons such as small knives. Sometimes people are cut deeply without even knowing that it has happened'. Quick and heavy sentencing has played a part in treating the scourge but it is clear that Leopold dislikes the restrictive measures that have become necessary... 'If two people cannot stand next to each other and enjoy a match, what on earth has society come to?' he said. 'If there is disorder, we must take positive action. The public of the West Midlands would not thank us for dealing with hooligans in a slack manner and that is why we have adopted such precautions as TV, dogs, shields, batons, mounted policemen, police escorts, body searches and so forth. We are society's dustmen.'

Five days after that feature appeared, the approval we were eagerly awaiting was finally given by the ACCs (Crime and Operations) for a joint uniform and CID operation to look at the Zulu Warriors and to obtain evidence to bring them before the courts. The staffing levels I had recommended were accepted and the starting date for the full-scale operation was to be 30 March, with an agreement to run it until some time in October 1987, the actual date to be determined by the evidence gathered and by Birmingham City's fixture list and so on. At last we were ready to go and I could start to put our plans into action. I was cautiously elated.

CHAPTER 5

US AND THEM

THE NUMBER OF police officers on duty for a football match hung on the history of the home and away support and the intelligence available for that fixture. It was difficult to enumerate because policing had to cover not only the football ground but also the city centre and the transport routes connecting the two. At the ground, officers would be deployed in phases of time to fixed locations before, during, and after the game. That might be turnstile duties for searching fans before entering the stadium, tunnel and line-side duties to ensure the safety of players and officials, traffic duties at key junctions, static deployments outside known trouble spots such as pubs, and attention to specific parts of the terraces.

Police managed the process through a Gold, Silver and Bronze structure, with a senior officer operating from what we called Alpha Control for significant matches. Gold was the overall command level, Silver the middle layer that implemented strategy by issuing tactical deployments to the Bronze commanders, and Bronze was where words were put into actions; where the rubber hit the road, so to speak.

Mobile resources – public order vans and dog vans – would escort groups of fans before and after matches and respond to trouble. This was normally the role of the Operational Support Unit, which during the game would be deployed as complete serials to troublesome parts of the crowd, ready to intervene early. Serials were small cohorts led always by a sergeant and which ordinarily stayed together in a defined area or for a defined role. They were usually made up of six or seven constables but the OSU serials were slightly bigger. Three serials made up a Public Order Support Unit, which would be commanded by an inspector. The OSU serials always moved together, like a seamless snake through crowds or in a solid mass if confronted.

Even for routine matches I would expect at least a hundred officers to be on football duties. For bigger games that would move up well into the hundreds. Mounted officers and dog handlers would contain and escort fans outside the ground and regulate supporters at turnstiles. Other officers performed detention and control room radio and CCTV duties. Where available, football spotters, who normally worked in pairs, mingled with the crowds.

For Operation Red Card, I always deployed the officers to certain places before, during and after the match in the same phased manner. Ordinarily, four would visit The Crown pub and two would cover the area around New Street Station. Our static observation point would be manned by me and the two spotters before the game, then during the match they would deploy in the ground in uniform and I would visit the control room. Football policing is complex. If you 'over-police', you waste money and resources which could be better used elsewhere. But if you 'under-police', you face a serious risk of disorder and of people getting hurt. The police manage sporting events based on a formula of risk and proportionality but it can often be a difficult call to make.

Drawing from the experience of other forces, and taking into account the fact that some of our targets were involved in other crimes, we agreed to involve other CID staff at the start of our operation. To this end, another Detective Sergeant, Steve Trenbirth, with extensive incident room experience, was made part of the team as the office manager, an ordinary title but a very important role. We had worked together before and although we were not initially close, I valued his judgement and his ability to stay outwardly calm and relaxed even in the most taxing of situations. He had a clinical approach to gathering evidence which was just what we needed, and a good sense of humour, especially after a couple of pints. Steve, however, wanted us to focus on the 'main men' whilst I steadfastly refused to consider anything less than lifting as many as we could find evidence to charge.

STEVE TRENBIRTH: I was nominated for the operation due to my major incident skills. I didn't have an option. Saturday afternoons were a nightmare, with the fans coming into town after matches and running amok. One Saturday I dealt with one job where some of them picked up a display fridge from an electrical shop which was next to Watches Of Switzerland in Corporation Street, and threw it through the window to have the watches away.

Two detective constables were taken on full-time to assist Steve in case-building and file preparation, one of them being DC Andy Murcott. Andy was twenty-eight at the time and had completed about six years' service. He had been on the CID for a year. Initially I had no doubt that the two DCs would have preferred to be tackling 'proper crime' and it took them a little while to understand the link between crime and public order, but I am quite sure the experience they gained was invaluable and mutually advantageous.

ANDY MURCOTT: Mike Layton rang me and asked me if I would be interested in working on the inquiry. I was at Digbeth CID at the time and had worked with Mike on the Shoplifting Squad. I thought, why not? In 1975 I had been at school with a Birmingham hooligan who used to show us a piece of wood with razor blades stuck in it which he said he took with him to games. He went on to study medicine at university. I thought that these were the sort of people that we would be dealing with.

The only female officer on the inquiry, WPC Gaynor Ball, was employed as an indexer. Gaynor was in many ways too nice to be a police officer. Always smiling, nothing was ever too much trouble for her, and in addition to her skills gained from working in major incident rooms she acted as a stabilising influence in the office and kept the team in order. There was definitely less bad language flying around when she was there and she was respected for being a hard worker. The job that she did had none of the glitz of the rest of the team but was

US AND THEM

still important to our success. She eventually married a senior officer and is now retired.

In our office we had dry-wipe boards and desks for briefing as well as cabinets to store paperwork and exhibits. If I don't have 'OCD' I certainly have the symptoms and needed to work in a totally tidy environment. Asking officers who we were expected to behave like slobs in their undercover roles to then comply with my fanatical neatness in the office was not without challenges, and the staff would occasionally hide my dry-wipe pens or rub things off the board, just to watch my loss of a sense of humour, which would be profound and lasting until order was restored. In pure management terms it was, and still is, highly inappropriate to swear at junior officers but there were times when I didn't stick to the management model.

This was to be the largest anti-hooligan operation ever undertaken in the UK, with more targets and more officers than any other. And it was to be renamed Operation Red Card, owing to a concern that Rourke's Drift was potentially racially insensitive. Although I didn't agree and saw it as over-sensitive political correctness, the new name certainly was more football-specific and therefore I suppose more appropriate. Officers would be drawn from three divisions, F, E and A (the Operational Support Unit), to involve thirteen officers full-time, six of them to be deployed as covert/undercover officers and two as overt spotters. The coverts were always to work in pairs. I considered putting them in threes but discounted it on the basis that it would be unwieldy in terms of evidence gathering, and the number of locations that we

105

could cover at any given time. They had different styles and attitudes to their work and as such would go on to achieve varying degrees of infiltration, some managing to observe activity from very close quarters whilst others were to work from a theoretically safer distance. I vowed to myself that I would not push them on this as long as I knew they were doing their best within their own individual limits; no 'cardboard cut-outs' here! For operational reasons I subsequently added a British Transport Police officer too.

The two overt spotters, Mark and Liam, were employed full-time in an open capacity, embracing some of the standard duties of football spotters as well as contributing significantly to the investigation in other ways. They would go on to more than prove their worth, often standing right in the heart of volatile crowds, two blue uniforms in a sea of animosity. They travelled to home and away games looking out for potential targets and making identifications by seemingly routine stop-checks on suspects. They were also able to offer a degree of protection to the covert officers by clandestinely and unob-trusively monitoring their movements, as well as keeping in touch by radio with me. I usually placed myself in the control room, where I could monitor CCTV and brief the local police commanders in real time if problems arose.

Both of these overt officers were very experienced in public order matters and adopted a no-nonsense approach to their work. If you were a suspect and you were playing up, you might get one chance to calm down and behave if warned. You wouldn't get a second one. They were to make a number of arrests during the operation, without compromising the operation as a whole. They were both controlled and fearless in these situations, and when the chin straps were down on their helmets and the black leather gloves went on no matter what the weather conditions, you knew they meant business. Mark was tall, extremely smart at all times in uniform, and very professional, especially when dealing with other police forces. He could be outspoken but I valued his opinions and held him in high regard. He had always followed Birmingham City as a supporter and was familiar with the ground, the environment and the history of hooliganism. I knew that he would advance in the service and indeed he did go on to achieve a senior rank within the CID in later years.

MARK: Mike [Layton] had a singular drive and determination to deliver this, and that was clear from the outset. The reality of the task sorted the doers from the talkers and some were genuinely brave. We were well organised and well led. My partner and I had the job of looking after the UC [under-cover] officers if all went badly, while gathering evidence of the overt acts of the hooligans. Disorder, apart from being occasionally scary, could be exciting and test your bottle. We hated quiet games! The team was unique as was the task, it was a good period of time and one I was genuinely glad to have experienced. The public seldom understand the confrontational nature of policing and in these times we fought for control, sometimes literally, of the streets. That much vaunted image of Dixon Of Dock Green was always nonsense, policing was about sorting out problems more than discussing them. I know that is not a universally held view, and there are examples of policing not getting it right, however this problem needed tackling not tickling. I learnt a lot that served me well later in service. Policing is not about making friends with either colleagues or communities, it is about pulling together and getting it done, take a deep breath and then on to the next issue. Not glamorous, not healthy, and definitely not good for marriages!

The second overt officer, Liam, also took a personal pride in his appearance and was a 'Jack the lad' with a healthy sense of humour, most of which related to home life and the routine ear-drummings that he received. His domestic updates often occupied the first few minutes of each day, a bit like a soap opera. He had a very easy style with football fans, who related well to him, but this belied a firm edge and attitude when needed. Whilst the first officer normally took the lead, they were a great partnership and just what I needed for the plans to proceed smoothly and efficiently.

LIAM: I had six years' service, twelve months of which were on the Operational Support Unit, on Delta Serial. Mark was also on that serial so I knew him well. I was originally nominated to do a covert role but before Operation Red Card started I had locked up 'Francis' for a public order offence and he was awaiting trial. It was just too risky, as I had got to know him well, so Alex and I swapped roles and he went undercover. We saw the same groups of hooligans causing problems every week so I wanted to be involved. I was also a true Blues supporter.

Four undercover officers came from the Operational Support Unit. Adam was tall, strong-jawed, physically fit and quietly confident in his abilities. He was intelligent but perhaps too prone to keep his own counsel.

ADAM: I was nominated for Operation Red Card by my Chief Inspector John Peake on the Operational Support Unit. He asked me in to his office and asked me to name three or four Birmingham City players. I didn't know much about football or Birmingham City; I was more of a rugby fan. I knew David Seaman, the goalkeeper, who went on to play for England. He asked me if I wanted to do some plain-clothes work and I said 'Yes' and that was it. John Peake was very supportive of me. Some time later I tried to withdraw from taking the inspectors' promotion examinations and he told me that I had missed the cut-off date to withdraw. I knew I hadn't and tried to protest but he took the report from his desk drawer and ripped it up in front of me and said, 'Get studying.' I passed by the skin of my teeth.

I partnered up with Colin. I had known him since joining the police and we lived in single men's quarters together. We were both on Uniform Bravo on the OSU. When we started we went out and had our hair bleached and highlighted and Colin had his ear pierced.

Colin was the more serious-looking of the four, with piercing eyes and strong views on life which sometimes led to, shall we say, challenging conversations. We did not always agree but that is not a criticism. He and Adam both took to wearing jeans and denim jackets for their undercover work and managed to blend well into the background. The covert officers were all different but all of them brought something invaluable to the party.

ALEX: I was originally supposed to be a uniformed spotter on the operation and not a covert officer but one of the other officers had arrested one of the main targets a few times before and we couldn't risk it. So we swapped roles. I'd damaged my right foot playing a friendly game of football just before the job was supposed to start and I had a plaster cast put on. Mike [Layton] made it clear that I wouldn't be able to do the job if I was limping around in plaster. So there was nothing for it: I went to the Accident Hospital and had the plaster cast taken off, against the doctor's advice. I didn't enjoy any of the undercover work but I wasn't there to live the role or to enjoy it, I was there to do a job and although I was bricking it, I was determined to finish it. Every day was a challenge in an alien environment. My partner Danny fitted in well with football hooligans but I didn't. I was nervous. But it was a job I wasn't going to walk away from.

COLIN: I went on the OSU in September 1985 and was there during the Handsworth riots. We used to do public order van patrols around the area of John Bright Street and the Edwards Number 7 Club in the city centre every Friday and Saturday night. It was known as Zulu territory and there were regular fights there and loads of arrests, lots of it Zulu-related. During Christmas 1986, we were doing covert patrols in Birmingham city centre trying to combat offences of 'steaming' and street robberies. I knew Harry Doyle [the officer injured in Boogies nightclub] and used to have a drink with him; I would describe him as a 'lively Irishman'. I was on B Serial of the Operational Support Unit. Paul Hartland was our sergeant at the time. He had me and Adam in to his office and said there was a 'little football job' coming up which would last for six weeks and were we interested? I said, 'Why not?' After that we met Mike Layton and he explained to us what the job was actually about and that it would involve undercover work. We both came away thinking, 'What have we let ourselves in for?' but still decided to go for it. When I realised it was Blues I was worried and thought that we would have difficulties because we were policing the football week in, week out and knew a lot of the hooligan element.

When I look back on the recruitment process, it had more in keeping with a music hall farce than a serious process based on relevant skills and experience or any account of the officers' character, knowledge and ability to cope under pressure. This was, however, how the police service often functioned and I was used to it. As a mere detective sergeant I wasn't in a position to debate with senior officers whether or not I would accept certain staff. I had to gamble that they had reluctantly given me some of their best officers rather than offloaded some of their worst. Events were to confirm it was much more of the former and any initial reservations I might have had soon diminished. There was a degree of 'who you know' rather than 'what you know' but none of us were perfect and we would just have to adjust to each other.

Basic terms of reference were drawn up and it was decided to give the team the name 'Special Operation Unit'. Apart from the normal administrative guidelines, there were also two key elements made explicitly clear to everyone involved: firstly, at no stage should any officer do anything which could be construed as inciting, aiding, abetting or counselling the commission of an offence (better known as agent provocateur behaviour), and secondly, if any covert officer was either identified or in danger of being identified, they should withdraw from the situation immediately. And if one covert team needed to help another in danger, then they should do so until other help arrived, even if it jeopardised the success of the operation. No matter how important this operation was, the safety of the staff and the public was paramount. Though we were all new to this type of work and would often have to make snap judgements, that particular rule always stood.

The original incident room was located on the first floor of a relatively quiet police station in a sparsely populated area. This was far from ideal, particularly for the undercover officers, but it had easy access at the back of the building and was in walking distance of Birmingham city centre and St Andrew's. No-one could enter the room other than members of the team, and a strict 'need to know' policy was enforced to protect the identities and activities of the covert officers. Contrary to what the public might think, police officers are not great at keeping their mouths shut and there are those who cannot help but gossip, so it was important that there was no loose talk.

In the later stages of the operation, owing to refurbishment it was necessary to move the incident room to a smaller location in a densely populated area, Bridge Street West Police Station, in Newtown, which was hardly perfect. We had no choice but to use the front door of these new premises to get in, although we had secure offices upstairs. This was a cause of considerable concern to our undercover officers, who ran the risk of bumping into people who could be answering bail at the station front desk. We were very fortunate that no-one was compromised but some of our potential targets lived in the area, a risk we would much rather not have taken. In truth it was a crazy situation which should have been unacceptable.

The whole team had the benefit of a day with our colleagues from the Metropolitan Police, where matters such as cover stories, false identities and forms of bogus identification for undercover work were discussed.

ANDY MURCOTT: They told us how easy it is to get close to the main targets: 'Just go to their pubs and to the grounds with them and they'll tell you what they've been up to and what they're planning to do.' But our experiences were to prove very different. We found that they [the Zulu Warriors] were a closed group, particularly the hardcore; they had known each other for many years and were reluctant to welcome outsiders. So our covert officers were only able to pick up snippets of conversation, which we then had to investigate.

ADAM: At the briefing we had with the Metropolitan Police they talked about the use of inappropriate nicknames for targets and said not to use things like 'JC' (Jesus Christ). One of them also talked about his partner, who had been some sort of public schoolboy. The message was: make sure you pick the right staff, because they were on the terraces one day with Chelsea and it started raining cats and dogs. This guy said in a posh accent, 'If it rains any more we will be playing water polo.' The undercover Met officer looked around at the supporters surrounding them and thought, 'Christ, we are in the shit.'

In reality I don't think my team gained that much from the interaction. I think that they viewed the Met officers with a degree of suspicion when they tried to make the undercover work sound easy. But it had to be done. The relationships between forces were not always warm and there were clear cultural and geographical differences between our officers and those from London. They were from the capital and we were from the 'second city'. There were bound to be differences in style and approach and one of my officers was to comment afterwards, 'Well that was a bit of a fucking waste of time.' We all went out for an Indian balti meal in a back street restaurant after the briefing and I wished the Met lads well in their endeavours. We would go on to chart our own territory.

Although their full names are not revealed here, for reasons of confidentiality and security, most of our coverts used their own first names while other personal details were falsified or amended. For instance, for their home addresses we used the right names of roads and Birmingham districts but never gave out a house number. Each officer developed his own cover story which they were thoroughly tested on, and carried such things as false UB40 benefit cards and fake copy charge sheets, letters regarding outstanding fines, and Birmingham City club membership cards. We created prison letters and letters from solicitors, and they carried betting slips and even condoms. All the items were designed to add to the coverts' credibility. At no time were they to carry their warrant cards; no wallets either, or cheque books or personal diaries.

The undercovers were to dress casually from now on, similar to the men they would be mixing with. To change their appearances as much as was believable, some got their ears pierced for earrings or studs, facial hair was cultivated and some grew their hair long. They were not a pretty bunch but this wasn't a fashion contest or a play, it was real life and very dangerous. We had to get it right and treat it all with steadfast seriousness. Each covert was to be tested by colleagues on his knowledge of Birmingham City too, such as fixtures and attendances at away matches, as we expected it to come in useful at some stage. They were instructed not to reveal their true identities to any person under any circumstances and one of my jobs was to check details of persons arrested both at home or away fixtures to ensure that none of our men had been arrested. If they were then they knew that they would just have to sit tight until I went to get them.

The safety of our officers of course was my primary concern, followed by preserving the integrity of any evidence gathered. We spent time talking about stress and I encouraged the officers to always be open and to share their feelings within the team. Most of them had wives or girlfriends and so I also urged them to be open with those closest to them too about what they were doing, though not in great detail. Extended family and friends were a different issue: each of the team created individual cover stories for close ones asking questions. And in the workplace we all entered a period of relative isolation from former colleagues. It was all strictly need-to-know; loose talk and idle chat were most certainly out.

We would brief and debrief the team in detail, going over and over different scenarios. It was always with their benefit in mind. As the operation proceeded, we would at times have lively discussions but when the time for debate was over they understood what the plan was and did their best to stick to it, knowing that I would be 'thoughtful' if they didn't. I was open to small compromises at times but this was to be no democracy and I expected people to follow instructions. We all came to know each other's weaknesses and strengths and we naturally supported each other, knowing that there was simply no formal training course available to teach officers how to act as football hooligans and that we were very much making it up as we went along. While we did have evidential and procedural rules to follow, we encountered a lot of 'suck it and see' scenarios which we simply had to make a snap judgement on. At the end of the day it was down to me to make sure that everything we did was legal, proportionate, and as safe as possible. The first was relatively easy to achieve, the second a matter of opinion and judgement, and the third impossible to guarantee.

CHAPTER 6

EYES AND EARS

GOOD QUALITY VISUAL evidence would be essential for Operation Red Card, we all knew that, but getting it would be difficult. I had already been to football grounds where the practice was to obtain a montage film of away supporters standing on the terraces. Some CCTV camera operators, though, would sweep the cameras across the crowds so quickly that clear enough detail was virtually impossible to glean, plus the viewer just about suffered motion sickness when trying to study it afterwards. At one ground I had to listen to an operator for two hours telling me the story of his life and how good he was. It didn't look to me as if he had been out on the streets for some time. Personally I would not have paid him in washers and the hooligans would have been highly amused to see the incompetent way in which the cameras were handled. He had been performing the role for some time and convinced his seniors that he was an expert, a fallacy that seemed to have been blindly accepted.

We planned everything in detail and scrutinised every aspect of our approach. For example, when considering how covert officers should travel to and from games, we decided that coach would be too restrictive. Most of our suspects avoided that form of travel because police forces dictated that coaches arrive just before, and leave as soon as possible after, each match. Hooligans did not appreciate this as it seriously hindered their hopes of fighting, so it then restricted our scope for evidence gathering. Travelling by train would allow the coverts to monitor people more closely, but their safety had to be considered, particularly in London where ambushes on the Underground by rival groups were not uncommon. Another factor to consider was the frequency with which small groups of supporters left trains before the actual destination to avoid the expected police escort to the ground or to meet rival gangs for prearranged fights. Driving by car also severely limited the coverts' ability to collect evidence, as they were advised not to give lifts to other supporters. This was to avoid any later claims that targets would not have been able to cause trouble had they not been given a lift by our officers; any allegations that we had acted as agents provocateurs would be extremely damaging to our case. I wanted to avoid coverts over-infiltrating the Zulus and engaging in criminal activities; they were there to carry out close surveillance and observation of suspects but that had to stop just short of close and direct association with them. Also on the matter of our coverts travelling to away games by car, we had to be sure that their vehicles were not identified and so instructed them to park some distance from the football ground. However, this in turn left them isolated when they left the match, as well as open to attack by opposing fans.

Each and every deployment would present us with health and safety challenges and the responsibility for making sure that no one got hurt rested with me. It wouldn't always be easy and there were to be times when I would simply be forced to take a calculated risk while needing to reassure staff that it would all be okay. These situations were often logistical nightmares but they had to be faced. There were always plenty of 'what if?' questions from the officers, and sometimes I simply had to draw a line on the conversations. Without a crystal ball I could not predict the outcome of everything.

When it came to going in pubs and socialising, the undercover men were encouraged to get to know bar staff well so that their faces became familiar, but not to invade people's personal spaces. If it was appropriate to do so, they should swear and be uncouth even if such behaviour was alien to their normal character. Eye contact with gang members ought to be avoided, as looking at the wrong person at the wrong time, perhaps at any time, could arouse suspicions. While on the terraces, the coverts were told to stand behind and to the left or right of targets so that they could watch and listen out for any useful information. Every fixture, home or away, had unique features to it. We had learned already that if the town or city of the next Birmingham away match on a Saturday was close to a coastal or holiday resort, supporters would often plan to travel on the Friday and return on the Sunday, staying in the resort and making a weekend of it. This of course increased the potential for alcohol fuelled disorder in those unlucky locations.

In keeping with other operations, officers were not given specific targets at the outset, to ensure that they did not adopt too narrow a view. From a safety perspective it was also vital that they were not made aware of the personal details of targets from within the incident room. For them to inadvertently start using the names of targets in public would inevitably raise questions as to how our men knew those names. Zulu Warriors would 'qualify' themselves as primary targets by virtue of the standard of evidence obtained against them as the operation progressed.

In the office, each target had an individually numbered folder containing various details and documents, including their real name or the nickname we had given them. Nicknames were often used because targets' real names weren't known and it would have been much too risky for undercover officers to try to find them out. In the folders would also be prisoner or surveillance photographs of the individual, their associates, previous convictions, a précis of incidents they had been involved in, and statements of evidence. It was important to gather details of the clothes they wore and of potential exhibits to recover when they were finally arrested in order to assist with identification and corroboration. Until we were absolutely sure of someone's identity, we referred to them only by designated police nickname, studiously avoiding adopting contentious or inappropriate names. This is how such character names as 'Elm' and 'Green Hood' originated. Elm was white, slim and tall, like an elm tree, while Green Hood usually wore the same coat which had, yes, a green hood. Elm was just seventeen years old and the sort of person who, rather than take an active part in violence, would run around excitedly at the rear, encouraging the front line to get stuck in, so to speak. Such behaviour can be almost as damaging as the fighting. Green Hood was white and twenty-two years of age, from Hodge Hill, Birmingham. He had a stocky build, fat face and short haircut. He seemed to be with Francis virtually all the time, leading us to rank him as a 'second lieutenant' to the gang leader. Elm would become target 10 and Green Hood target 2

The individually numbered folders formed the basis of our early discussions with the Crown Prosecution Service. We were provided with two dedicated contacts, Desmond Jaggers and Paul West, who from the outset were both enthusiastic and constructive. The relationship between the police and the CPS has not always been smooth but these two prosecutors were first class from day one, and while they never lost their focus on evidence as opposed to conjecture, they were very committed to us getting a good result, and dare I say it, even got excited at times as they watched events unfold, rather a change from their normal position of waiting to be presented with a case file. They would also help manage some delicate situations where our covert officers were due to give evidence at court in previous, unconnected cases they had been involved in. Simply walking into the court public areas could pose a real threat of exposure if nothing was done to prevent it.

We categorised the gang into groups, namely mainstream Zulu Warriors, the B Team and what we called the 'Up-and-Comers'. We made up the B Team name ourselves. They were a distinct group who we identified as being involved in hooliganism at an early stage but did not seem to be directly linked to the mainstream Zulus. The Up-and-Comers included a pack of youths trying to make a violent reputation for themselves, namely the self-titled Junior Business Boys, presumably so called because they were younger than the main Zulus and because they 'did the business'. To help provide a clearer picture for our officers, I issued a relatively simple description of the hooligans' overall structure: like that of an apple, with an outer skin, a middle part and a core. The mainstream Zulus were the core and, of course, we considered them as rotten.

It was clear that they worked within a tribalistic system involving close relationships and a hierarchy as well as loose affiliations. This allowed them to operate in small, tight-knit groups while also at times being able to call on several hundred peripheral members. Some targets probably did not know each other and perhaps had never even met each other before, yet they adopted the same common causes of violence, disorder and promoting the Zulu Warriors. Whilst not unique, what also made them stand out in those days was the gang's diversity. The Zulu Warriors comprised men from a variety of ethnic backgrounds including those of West Indian origin as well as mixed race, British Asian, and white British. This contrasted starkly with rival 'firms', many of whose members were white and had extreme right-wing views. What we did notice, however, throughout the course of Operation Red Card was a complete lack of women in or with the gang.

As well as being a regular drinking venue for normal supporters, The Crown was, as mentioned, one of the Zulus' main meeting places. Some of the older Blues group who used the pub were more heavy drinkers and idiots than hooligans or hardened Zulus, though a few of them needed very little encouragement to join in any fights. A number of those individuals had also been involved in 'strimming' fruit machines before – stealing cash out of the gambling machines using certain clever devices to do so via the coin slot. On one occasion they had even gone out of town to go strimming, visiting Stratford-upon-Avon to 'do' some of the pubs there. Nevertheless, Operation Red Card was chiefly concerned with the activities of the Zulu gang and so it seemed obvious that our cause would benefit if we could somehow put clandestine officers in or at least near to the pub.

*

On Saturday, 21 March, a uniformed permanent beat officer was on his daily patrol near The Horsetrader pub in Smallbrook Queensway. The pub was small, facing a dual carriageway, and only a short distance from New Street Station. This area was the officer's patch and he was well acquainted with the residents, the licensees, the shopkeepers and of course the local criminals. Shortly before 1 p.m., he noticed a group of youths trying to force their way past the doorman into the pub. At the front of the mob was one of Operation Red Card's main targets, given the name Francis by the task force. The youths failed to enter The Horsetrader and so ran off to regroup outside The Crown in Hill Street. The beat officer followed, determined to intervene as well as to stop-check Francis. This he managed to do with relative ease, though it would emerge later that Francis gave him an array of false details. Francis was a quietly spoken individual but it was clear he wasn't lacking in confidence and cunning, or a lust for violence.

Birmingham City were due to play at home versus Portsmouth and scores of away supporters had already arrived in the city. As a consequence, the natives were getting excited. Arriving early was a familiar tactic adopted by football gangs hoping for combat and today the Zulus and associates were relishing the day ahead against the visiting supporters. Their hostility towards the Portsmouth followers may have been reinforced by recent press reports of racially motivated violence committed by 'a gang of white Portsmouth soccer thugs' raiding a club largely used by Caribbean members of the local Derby community. The incidents took place before the Derby County versus Portsmouth Division Two match. The yobs smashed windows of the Texas Goldmine Social Club, wrecked nearby property and set a car on fire. Twenty Portsmouth fans were arrested.

By 1.20 p.m., there was a large gathering of men outside The Crown, including a number of known Zulus. Although Operation Red Card had only recently begun, the police were aware of, and had information on, certain faces – even if their real names were not yet known – who were recognised as being part of the Zulu gang already from intelligence reports or previous convictions. In small groups, the men began making their way towards Smallbrook Queensway and then into Ladywell Walk. Francis was among them. They were being followed on foot by a few police officers. By now Portsmouth supporters had congregated in the bar area of The Fox pub in Hurst Street, joining regular customers already drinking there.

Shortly before 1.30 p.m. some of the Portsmouth supporters were standing close to the entrance door of the pub and in sight of people outside the premises. Outside, Zulu chants suddenly rose, increasing in intensity and threat. Then dozens of Zulus suddenly surged towards the doorway, led by an Asian-looking youth brandishing a knife with a folding blade. The Portsmouth fans immediately retreated into the pub, many of them to behind the interior bar, throwing beer glasses at their attackers to try to ward them off.

The pub was then hit by a bombardment of missiles, which smashed most of the windows and caused an estimated £2,000-worth of damage. A gas canister was tossed into the pub by one of the Birmingham gang, causing nausea and distress to the people inside. Injuries were reported, as well as effects of the gas, but none of them were deemed serious. Police officers arriving on the scene managed to make one arrest, for criminal damage (our later target 'Fife'), but the Zulus dispersed. Minutes later, more fighting occurred in Edgbaston Street close by and two further arrests for public order offences were made: a twenty-five-year-old white man from Sutton Coldfield who we called 'Robin', and 'Frank'. Other Red Card targets known to be involved in these particular incidents were Francis, Green Hood, 'Milk Race', 'Sidekick', 'Red', 'Light', 'Shirt Out', 'Wax', 'Gingerbeard', 'Fossil', plus a twenty-year-old from Castle Bromwich who we christened 'Rooky'.

Milk Race was an interesting character. Of West Indian origin, he was a slim nineteen-year-old from Bordesley Green. He wore large, gold-rimmed spectacles, had short black curly hair and sported a small moustache. He was regularly seen in a white Milk Race cycling type of cap, a dark blue tracksuit which had bottoms with white piping on, and a brown leather jacket. Being close to Francis and Green Hood marked him out as another second lieutenant of the Zulus. Target number 21, the gang's unofficial photographer, Shirt Out, was a slim, white, twenty-two-year-old from the Rubery area. He always seemed to wear a baseball cap with studs in and a green jacket, and whilst we did not see him fight he did take many action photos of others with his camera.

Although these incidents were not filmed, during the course of the day police video footage captured gang members outside The Crown, at New Street Station and at St Andrew's. Much of it was taken by West Midlands Police in the Hoolivan. All of it would come in very useful for the operation as certain known faces were identified while other target files were opened as a result of the day's activities.

In any large scale police operation, the likelihood of suspects evading arrest is high. Getting away with it is often more about their good fortune than bad police work. When we saw someone committing an offence, especially someone on whom we had good intelligence data, we gave them a nickname if we didn't know who they were and created a folder to put in everything relating to them, such as witness statements and photographs. Each folder was given a number and we ended up with at least seventy-five of them. In some cases, however, we only ever saw the suspects once or their faces on videotape or still photos which were not clear enough for identification. If that was the case, so be it; it was the end of that particular matter. Equally, if the intelligence we had gathered on them did not lead to actual evidence that was also the end of it. There were also instances of targets being in prison serving sentences for other offences, so in a certain respect they were lucky because their time in jail meant they were temporarily off our radar.

One of the more prominent black Zulus, Barrington Patterson, had his own account of being in the gang published in his 2013 book One-Eyed Baz. Officer Ian Mabbett had encountered him before.

IAN MABBETT: I knew One-Eyed Baz well. He was a black guy who used to come down on to New Street Station after matches had finished with a group of mixed black and white youths. You could tell some of them were just hangers-on. One of the group ['Harry', Red Card target 41] I also knew well. They used to split up and wander around the station concourse to see who was coming through. I was working with Paul Majster then, in the mid to late 1980s, and every Saturday the CID used to go down at 5 p.m. on the station in jeans and T-shirts to monitor the crowds of football fans. We often had prisoners for public order because we were able to get closer to them than the uniform staff. Depending on who was playing at Birmingham you would also get the Zulus running in through the glass doors chanting 'Zulu, Zulu'.

We had an offence called 'trespass and refuse to quit' in those days and we used to tell the regulars to clear off otherwise they would be arrested. Generally speaking, One-Eyed Baz, who often wore a deerstalker hat, would just smile and go when told but Harry was a different matter and would argue. Paul nicked him one day for threatening behaviour on the concourse and I gave him a hand to get him up to the British Transport Police office. He was mouthing off all the way up but not violent. When we got in to one of the detention rooms, he refused to be searched and suddenly grabbed Paul around the throat and went berserk. I had to hit him with my truncheon to make him break his hold.

I remember another occasion when Blues were on the station at the same time as Cardiff and West Ham, all passing through. It all cracked off as they mixed up together and all the panic alarms in the booking office started going off at the same time. It was bedlam. I also knew a white guy called Paul who was a Rod Stewart lookalike and used to come on to the station and ask the staff for train times for arriving fans. Years later I met him in the Yard Of Ale pub in New Street with his wife. We got chatting and he told me that he had been one of the leaders of the Zulus. Knowing what I knew I didn't believe him, but I was happy to let him carry on boasting. He told me that he had received word about the football operation and went to stay in Nottingham for a while, out of the way. I have no doubt that he was a spotter for the gang but I put the rest down to what he read in the newspapers.

Another one who used to come on regularly was a white youth we called 'Stretch' – he was about six foot seven tall. A lot of the Zulus used to drink in the Bar St Martin, which was at the bottom of the Rotunda building and had been called the Mulberry Bush at the time of the IRA pub bombings in 1974, when a bomb went off inside. I knew the licensee, Pat, well; he was a no-nonsense Irishman who threw people out for the slightest bit of trouble. I used to drink at one end of the bar and the Zulus would be at the other end. It was one big room. They knew who I was but they left me alone because I knew the licensee, and I left them alone. A number of the Zulus got jobs as doormen in the pubs and clubs in Birmingham city centre.

*

The trial of the so-called Chelsea Headhunters ended that May after a marathon eighteen weeks, to considerable press attention. A culmination of the Metropolitan Police's lengthy Operation Own Goal, it was hailed initially as a major success. Two men, Terry Last and Stephen Hickmott, who were said to be the gang's leaders, were each jailed for ten years, while three others received shorter sentences. (It didn't look quite as successful when, a couple of years later, the convictions were quashed after doubts were raised over the police methods of collecting information, and a couple of similar trials collapsed.)

Coincidentally, a casual discussion of that initial trial led to an incident that starkly brought home to my team the dangers inherent in the undercover investigation of such dangerous gangs.

ADAM: Not long after starting, it was a sunny day and me and Colin had been deployed to the city centre. There was a pub near to John Bright Street with some tables outside. We sat down to have a beer and there was nothing particularly going on. A couple of targets then arrived and we decided to stay and have another beer. Within ten minutes it was like a meeting had been arranged and a large group materialised and took over the seats and pavement, with us in the middle. They were all sat around us. All of the main players were there. One of them, a black guy, sat shoulder to shoulder with Colin reading The Sun newspaper about the Chelsea operation. They were chatting about it and Francis was also there. Somebody said, 'Do you think that they will ever do it to us?' The black guy said, 'No. No chance there. There are not enough black coppers in the West Midlands Police to get into the Zulus.' Unfortunately, his comment was a fairly accurate one, not that there was anything I could do about the issue at the time.

COLIN: We were sat amongst fifty to sixty Zulus, all talking about the Chelsea undercover operation. It was the day of the Shrewsbury game at Birmingham on 9 May, the last match of the season in fact. We were sat in the sunshine outside Edwards Number 7 in John Bright Street. Two very attractive women walked up and sat nearby. I would say it was mother and daughter. Adam went inside to get another drink. I started to hear someone calling out my real first name and I tried to ignore it. It was the elder of the two women. She started to try to talk to me and I tried to ignore her but she insisted on repeating my name. I told her that she had got the wrong person but she said, 'You are a policeman aren't you?' The world stood still for me. I gave her a load of abuse and swore at her and told her to fuck off. I walked straight inside to get Adam and told him that we had to go straight away. We left the drinks at the bar, walked through the crowd and turned a corner and legged it as fast as we could. I couldn't work out who she was, then realised that in 1982 to 1985 I was at Kings Heath and we used to have a tea spot at Moseley Hall Hospital. She worked on the reception there. We phoned Mike to tell him what had happened. I deeply regret the way I swore at her but we were very lucky.

CHAPTER 7

HILL STREET BLUES

SOMETIMES THE LEVEL of violence meted out by the Zulus was frightening. One example encountered by our undercover officers came in April 1987 after a match against Oldham Athletic at their Boundary Park ground. The result was a 2–2 draw. Covert Alex recalls what happened afterwards.

ALEX: There was a good sized group of Birmingham supporters at Werneth Railway Station and the police had just left us there. In our group was a young mixed-race lad, well over six foot tall, who smiled a lot but knew how to handle himself if he needed to, which is why we nicknamed him 'Bruno', after the boxer Frank Bruno. A small group of Oldham suddenly appeared on the old stone bridge in the roadway above and started giving the 'come on'. They must have been mad as they were well outnumbered. Everyone just charged at them and one or two Oldham slipped over as people were running around. They were attacked. Several Birmingham grabbed hold of one of them off the floor and started to lift him up. We honestly believed that they were going to throw him off the bridge onto the train line. It was pretty scary. We had to do something and one of us shouted, 'Train!' They dumped him in the road and everyone legged it down to the platform. Fortunately for us a train did come shortly after.

Known B Team targets involved in the attack were Goofy, Baby Face and Sleepy. Five people, including Bruno, would subsequently be charged with violent disorder over this incident. One of them, Dal, a white twenty-five-year-old from Lea Village in Birmingham, who was employed as a setter, was later fined for affray. The fact that they were classed as B Team members clearly did not make them any the less dangerous than fully-fledged Zulus.

Following the fighting at Werneth, the Birmingham hooligans travelled the few miles to Manchester Victoria Station by train, looking for more prey, this time in central Manchester. No discrimination, they would fight or simply set about anyone they could, regardless of football or territorial affiliations, if any. Everyone was fair game and if innocent bystanders were involved or affected then tough shit for them, they shouldn't have been there. The yobs' aim of more confrontation that day was achieved: skirmishes and fights broke out with local youths, football teams unknown, until police arrived to escort them back to Piccadilly Station for their belated return journey to the Midlands.

The following Saturday, 11 April, Tottenham Hotspur were due to play Watford at Aston Villa's ground in one of the football season's two FA Cup semi-finals. The semi-finals are always held at neutral venues and Villa Park was a frequent choice. Before the match, supporters from both teams were drinking in the city centre, as were the Zulus even though Birmingham City were not playing that day. A large number of them gathered at The Crown, its proximity to the railway station enabling the gang's spotters to keep watch for opposing gangs arriving by train and then to quickly tell the core leaders back at the pub. Inside The Crown we had two of Red Card's covert officers, Alex and Danny. Two black bouncers regularly manned the doors. With their Afro hair styles, black suits, white shirts and black bow ties, they certainly looked the part but rarely did they make efforts to actually control the pub's clientele. The reality too was that many of the men frequenting The Crown never actually made it to Blues matches yet claimed to be a part of the nefarious activities in the name of the football. Our two undercovers had strict instructions to simply observe, to merge in to the crowd in The Crown and to stay in the background. Under no circumstances were they to engage in any criminal activity and if they felt there was trouble ahead then they should leave the premises and one of them put a baseball cap on his head as a signal to the police camera crew secretly situated in the first floor office opposite.

ALEX: The Crown was rammed with a lot of people going out scouting and loads of chatter. We were stood at the bar trying to listen to what was going on. Someone said something and we went outside.

Together with other officers on the operation, I had taken up a position in the office overlooking The Crown. In addition to a normal stills camera we were using a Panasonic CCD (charge-coupled device) video camera with a time and date stamp that was being trialled by the Home Office Research Unit. It supposedly gave greater image definition of moving targets. This theory would soon be tested. The officers were self-trained on the equipment, not the ideal strategy but strict time constraints meant appropriate training in photography was very limited. After any filming, all videotapes were to be immediately copied and sealed; they were not going to risk valuable evidence being wiped or chewed up in a tape machine. Anyone touching the originals again did so at their peril. The windows in the office had metal Venetian blinds which provided the police a small degree of protection from view, a priority, but they also made it difficult to get clear shots with the cameras. It all added to the tension for the officers in that building. They were too close for comfort to their targets. If they were seen then the consequences would be serious: the hunters would suddenly become the hunted.

The Crown was becoming increasingly crowded inside and out, and as more men gathered, four of them walked away towards a black two-door Mini car nearby, parked on double yellow lines next to a queue of black taxi cabs. The number plate was clearly visible and we were in play for a Police National Computer check which would give us the details of the recorded owner. They got into the vehicle, the driver a white youth wearing a black leather jacket, a black crew neck jumper and a gold necklace. He became the operation's target number 6, predictably given the name of 'Mini Driver'. One of the quartet was a slender black youth, his slightly too long, cream coloured, buttoned-up raincoat making him look out of place. He certainly did not feel out of place though: one main appeal of being in a football gang, the football gang, was the mutual feeling of camaraderie, common purpose, respect and feeling tough, even invincible. And the whole rush. He was target number 5, given the name of 'Raincoat'; and he sat in the front passenger seat. The two other youths sat in the back. One was short in height, wearing a greyish cagoule and blue jeans turned up at the bottom, and the other wore a dark jacket with a hood with a yellow lining in it. Unbeknown to us at this stage, they drove only a short distance to another pub in the area, the Craven Arms, to meet some Tottenham Hotspur followers. There, these 'ambassadors' for the Zulus delivered an invitation to their London rivals and an imminent meet was arranged. The stage was being set.

A few minutes later, the Mini returned and the driver and three passengers got out of the car and reported to Francis standing outside the pub entrance. Francis, our top target, was a stocky, twenty-one-year-old black man, quietly spoken but an intense individual and possessor of a most intimidating stare. His grey-and-black striped coat, buttoned up to the neck, made his frame look even larger.

There was a real mix of people at The Crown before the game at Villa Park, and while we were confident that we had some of our core targets there from the main Zulu group, there were younger affiliated elements present too, some of them Junior Business Boys, as well as a few regulars and hardened drinkers from the pub. We could tell that a large-scale disturbance was brewing and we had a hell of a job just identifying known targets in amongst the numerous others participating or at least in attendance. We would eventually spot, film, photograph and identify nearly forty of our eventual targets in this one incident, including not just Zulu leaders but some of the Junior Business Boys too.

By 1.17 p.m. our two covert officers had left the pub and were standing outside on a small traffic island which connected two zebra crossings across the road. The two were jamming baseball caps on their heads as often as they could and Danny was smoking cigarettes incessantly too to complement the message. They even put the cap on the heads of a couple of our targets, including the man in the grey-and-black striped coat. 'We wanted to make sure that the officers in the obs point were getting our message,' said Alex. 'We started pratting about, putting the cap on each other as well as on Francis and Elm.' Fortunately they didn't take offence. From our hidden location I called the Divisional Control Room, known as Foxtrot One, on the radio to warn them: 'DS Layton to Foxtrot One, there are some indications of some trouble occurring in the near future. I will let you know as soon as anything positive arises.' The problem still of course was that despite the efforts of the two coverts, we did not know exactly where and when the trouble was going to happen. It was absolutely clear that a fight was going to take place, but we needed more detailed information to substantiate it.

A man and a woman walked onto the zebra crossings and passed within a foot of some of our targets and the two undercover officers. They had two very small children with them, each child holding the man's hand and swinging their free arms happily. More seconds ticked by, then two teenage boys carrying plastic shopping bags stepped over the crossing followed soon after by a group of three women and two men slowly walking up towards Hill Street, more innocent civilians in the wrong place at the wrong time, entering the eye of a potentially dangerous storm and all of them Birmingham citizens for whom the Zulu Warriors had no regard.

Just then, our target Francis ran back to the pub to call everyone out. The fight was on.

At 1.20 p.m., a large number of Tottenham supporters, known as the 'Yids', their self-adopted nickname, were making their way from the Craven Arms towards New Street Station. When they reached Hill Street, many of the Birmingham crowd emerged from The Crown, chanting 'Zulu' and generally looking very agitated. On seeing the Tottenham contingent, they charged en masse towards them.

LIAM: I was in the office with Mike and Mark. We were never really shown how to use the camera and when it kicked off we wanted to get out there. It was a well-organised knock and Francis was right at the front.

As we watched from the office, struggling to get good views without revealing our position to the mob outside, Mark, one of the two overt officers with me, shouted, 'There are kids with knives.' I radioed the controller again as the team tried to get as much evidence as possible, with difficulty as the Venetian blinds clattered and clashed together as we tried to get the lenses of the cameras between its strips. To add to our frustration, most of the fighting was about to happen in an area to our left, adjacent to the road leading up to New Street Station, our view being partially obscured owing to the design of the building we were in. As soon as the fighting started, one of my team shouted, 'Get your camera going, Mick,' at which precise point the film on the stills camera ran out!

We saw two surges forward from the home mob, flashes of arms raised and people striking out in all directions. As the combat continued, we found it difficult to obtain good video images of the chaos. We did our best to get the visual evidence while trying to shout updates on the radio at the same time. It became pretty stressful inside that office, though nothing compared to events outside of course.

Like many such mêlées, the whole thing was over in a couple of minutes. In thugs' parlance it was 'a good row', with fighting involving over a hundred men at various spots in the area. A 'good row' it may well have been but within that maelstrom, a fifteen-year-old from Battersea, London, was stabbed in the stomach, and it was a life-threatening wound. It was hard for me to imagine a boy still of school age travelling to a football match intending to fight but then again it was fair to question what such a lad was doing consorting with a mob involved in a pre-arranged fight. As was often the case with football gang warfare, some maniacs never knew when to stop. One or two went too far here and nearly ended a life in doing so, in this case a mere boy's, all allegedly in the name of sports rivalry.

Mark, in the office, confirmed that he had seen 'the kid' who stabbed the Tottenham victim but it had not been possible to capture it on film. Colin, who was close to the scene, recalled.

COLIN: I cannot be one hundred per cent sure but my recollection is that the person who stabbed the Tottenham fan at the fight in Hill Street was a big Blues fan who worked in a cinema near The Crown. He did the stabbing and basically went back in to work so he would have been off the streets in seconds.

By sheer good fortune, a charge nurse from Selly Oak Hospital was driving his wife and young daughter through the city centre at the time. Without any thought for his own personal safety, he leapt out of the car and ran to provide first aid to the stricken youth, even as others were still trying to beat the lad as he lay on the ground in agony. The nurse's wife later told reporters, 'They carried on kicking him even though he was bleeding and my husband was begging with them to stop.' Some of the mob even began rocking the nurse's car with his wife and young daughter inside. Terrified, his wife placed their child in the rear of the car and covered her head with a blanket. Thankfully, arriving police officers restored order and drove off the mob. A police dog handler helped the nurse tending to the stab victim, making an urgent radio call for an ambulance, a call that was recorded: 'Foxtrot Delta One, this is an ambulance request, very urgent, we have someone stabbed, there's someone out there who is running around with a very big blade.' By this time the hairs were starting to stand up on the back of my neck.

A public order van, or Uniform Juliet, soon reached the scene with sirens blaring, causing the opposing mobs to disperse. They left the road littered with billiard cues and pool balls, coshes, metal bins and even road cones. Many of the culprits ran back into the sanctuary of The Crown, shaking hands with colleagues as they went, free from the attention of the police who knew better than to dash headlong into such a hostile environment with minimal back-up. I knew Neil, a sergeant who attended, quite well and also knew that if there were prisoners to take he would be leading from the front. Unfortunately I knew that he would have struggled today and it was far too early in Operation Red Card for us to reveal ourselves. Our main target, Francis, was actually spoken to by police officers on the ground but by this time he was acting out his role as an inquisitive member of the public wondering what all the fuss was about.

ALEX: The fight was over in minutes and after the stabbing it was all a bit of a shock. I thought, God this is for real. We went back into the pub afterwards and it was buzzing with the excitement of it all. Everyone was bragging and boasting and buoyed up by it all.

ADAM: On the day of the fight in Hill Street we were in The Crown earlier. My memory is that it was really busy and there were actually a couple of Tottenham fans in there but they were not risk fans and everyone ignored them. We stayed for a while and then went off in to the city and missed the fight, which we were annoyed about. We used to flirt with one of the barmaids in The Crown just to give us a bit of cover. She was a white girl, brunette, in her twenties and attractive. We did it so that she would remember us but we had to be careful because she was the girlfriend of one of the black doormen. We had to learn not to look around when we went in there as only police officers did that, so we would force ourselves to go up to the bar and order a drink and not look. There was no 'please' and 'thank you'.

The afternoon's events reinforced my view of how the hooligans structured themselves. Ironically, in some ways they mirrored the activities of the police with their use of intelligence gatherers, spotters (or 'loafers') and photographers, and a command structure and hierarchy. Their hardcore elements were committed to violence and hand-to-hand engagement with their rivals while the next layer, including the Junior Business Boys, wasn't as well defined. These people appeared happy to fight when the odds were in their favour and possibly depending on how much booze they had drunk. And the outer layer of the mob consisted of individuals who craved a sense of belonging and excitement. These people could be seen 'shaping' and doing a lot of running around at the back of the action but with little actual involvement in any fighting. The thing that bonded them all on such occasions was the Zulu chant, designed to put fear into the minds of opponents. I cannot imagine it not succeeding. Just as in the Zulu film, the chants were a preparatory act to moving forward to engage in combat. And in terms of tactics, the Zulu Warriors had the advantage of speed and mobility over the police who, deployed in vans and cars, inevitably were often chasing shadows.

At the debrief session later that day in the incident room of the police station, we had plenty to talk about and a lot of evidence to preserve. After the high-adrenalin day we had all experienced, people were tired and wanting to either relax, sleep or go for a drink. In addition to their stressful work-load, the undercover officers also had had to walk back to the station clandestinely. They were both physically and mentally fatigued, and the room would become hot and stuffy as people were coming to terms with the fact that this was not going to be fun. We had already nominated a 'safe' pub where we could retire to relative security but the pub visit had to wait, as all statements of evidence had to be completed at the earliest opportunity, no matter how long it took. All of the statements were checked to make sure that they bore signatures on every page, mistakes were initialled and correct dates, page numbers and the right timings were inserted. It was laborious and time-consuming, with officers hunched over tables, some chewing the ends of pens, trying to remember every little detail, slurping from ever-present mugs of tea and coffee to keep them going. Heads were scratched and eyes looked up to the ceiling searching for inspiration.

Each statement bore a witness caption, which had to be signed indicating that the statement was true to the best of their knowledge and belief and that you would be liable to prosecution if you had wilfully stated in it anything which you knew to be false. We only dealt in facts, it was that simple. We all made statements whether it was witnessing incidents or exhibits. For instance, each video tape and each camera film was numbered for continuity of evidence purposes. This was all mundane but all vital, the sort of detail that defence solicitors would pore over in hope of finding faults, regardless of how minute or seemingly trivial. No evidence is trivial in a court of law but if it isn't perfect then it can easily be rejected, deleted and struck from the record. We had no room for error, everything had to be right. Those were the rules and they were the rules for good reason and not just pedantic, bureaucratic demands. I had no intention of losing court cases on legal technicalities or lack of professionalism on our part. This meant my treading a careful line with the team as I wanted to be accessible to them at all times for welfare reasons but there again, my becoming 'one of the boys' would be a disaster. Being popular was not on my list of priorities. The Hill Street stabbing was very serious and if the young Tottenham fan died it would be, bluntly speaking, game over not just for the victim but also figuratively for everyone identified at the scene who would have to be arrested and might consequently be embroiled in a murder case. So we had to be meticulous. We had to get everything right. Everything.

There was one aspect of the incident which in hindsight we found amusing but which at the time brought home how precarious these fast-moving undercover operations can be, and how slender is the thread by which they often hang. One of the officers called out to quell the fighting was the experienced sergeant I have called Neil, who actually knew many of the Red Card team by sight.

SERGEANT NEIL: At that time I was running a squad at Steelhouse Lane police station in the city centre that dealt with volume crime and was completely different from dealing with public order matters. That afternoon I was in uniform on patrol in the city centre when a call came over the radio reporting trouble in the Hill Street area, near The Crown pub.

As I approached the pub, I could see another disturbance down the road, but before I had time for anything else, a number of youths burst out of the door of The Crown looking for trouble. In the group I spotted two who I knew to be police officers, in plain clothes. I had opened my mouth to say 'What are you doing here?' to one of them when he gave me a split-second glance that if translated into English would have said, 'Fuck off!' It was at that point I realised they were two of the Red Card undercover officers.

Within a millisecond, all sorts of stuff was going through my mind, like, have I blown his cover? Did anyone see our eyes meet? Have I just blown a very expensive undercover police operation? So in another millisecond I formulated a plan and kicked the u/c officer up the backside. Now don't get me wrong, this was not a regular thing I did to members of the public but it seemed a good idea at the time. I'm not sure the u/c operative thought that but it put him squarely back on the side of the Zulus. Normality was properly resumed some moments later when I arrested another youth who ran past me shouting, 'Get the cunts!' So no harm done – or so I thought.

On the following Monday morning, when I got a phone call from Mike Layton, I realised it wasn't quite the end of the matter. It transpired that others on the Red Card team had been covertly filming and had filmed me doing a good impression of trying to dropkick the u/c operative back into the pub. Oh great, I thought, just what I need. It's on film. However, there was a bit more and it transpired that an assistant chief constable, keen to see how his budget for the operation was being spent, decided he wanted to look at the covert film footage from the previous Saturday. Having watched it, he was a little bit dismayed to see one of his uniform sergeants kicking a member of the public up the arse. Fortunately, Mike had worked out what had happened during the incident and explained that the member of the public was in fact a u/c operative and it was all part of the plan. I think that placated him a little bit. Mike and I had a chuckle about that.

As for the u/c operative, I saw him later and we both agreed it was a bit close. I had to put my hand in my pocket and buy a few beers.

Although it was not discussed at the debrief, nor indeed would I have tolerated any discussion, the question must have been on some people's minds as to whether we could, or should, have stopped the fight taking place. It was my decision and in the final analysis there is no right or wrong in these situations. I might have had time to get police officers to stand outside The Crown in uniform, but would they have stopped a hundred people determined to fight or would they have simply moved them on to another street, which we were not covering, and therefore lose any chance of gathering visual evidence? One person was seriously injured, which was one too many, but how many people did we save from injury as a result of having the evidence to put some of these people away and to deter others? Hindsight is, as they say, a wonderful thing and things can look entirely different when analysed from the warmth of an armchair. Playing safe and avoiding risk was not my style. I had a small window of time to make a decision to disrupt the hooligans or to let things run, and such decisions are not for the faint-hearted, as they can be career changing. Looking back from the distance of time, would I do the same? Without a doubt I would. That doesn't mean I was right, it just means that someone had to take responsibility.

Crucially, our video and photographic evidence, as imperfect and chaotic as it had been to get, gave us a guarantee of success which enabled me to promise firm results to my senior managers. From the images collected, together with the statements gathered, we would be able to charge well over twenty individuals with the specific offence of violent disorder. Many of them were key players within the Zulu Warriors. We spent hours subsequently reviewing the video, cataloguing clothing and the actions of individuals. The evidence chain was coming together and we were confident it would prove to be of immense value in future court proceedings. Years later, one of the Zulus would remark that the 'dirty, no-good Yids' helped ensure Zulus were arrested by making statements to the police, but our own evidence was the most important in helping us seal those arrests.

We used something called a Tamron machine to print still images from the material, thus saving huge amounts of time and money. There was also a special video player with a dial that enabled us to watch the tape in slow motion as well as freeze frame, which improved our capacity to see the finer details that are missed when watching in normal time. This was 1980s technology. When we viewed the tapes, we established that a minimum of twenty-four people were seen to leave through the front door of The Crown as the fight started. We identified twenty-seven people who were later charged for their involvement. We also researched a further eleven people but were never able to positively identify them, even though they were definitely a part of the gang. In all, this meant that at least thirty-eight Zulus were involved in this fight.

It was, in a certain way, a good day for us and a bad day for them, though it would be some time before they realised it. We were all thankful that the Tottenham boy did not die, though I feel sure that some of the hooligans would have disagreed with me on that. I now knew that we would definitely be going to have our day in Crown Court with some of the key Zulu targets. The overt officers had also experienced a very busy day, not only with the observations at Hill Street but with two arrests made at Villa Park, one for threatening behaviour and another of a person who was already wanted on a warrant.

Later that evening, in an unrelated incident which we were not present to witness, the centre of Solihull saw what was described as a pitched battle between local Birmingham supporters and about thirty Watford fans outside the Snooty Fox pub. Bricks, beer glasses and bottles were thrown and an eighteen-year-old from St Albans was arrested for criminal damage. According to a press report the hooligans 'turned the centre of Solihull into a battleground hours after the FA

Cup semi-final at Villa Park'. Police were forced to seal off the street for more than forty minutes and several youths were treated for cuts and wounds caused by flying missiles until police dispersed the gangs. 'Police made seventy-nine arrests in total at the Tottenham v Watford game on Saturday – 51 before the match, 24 during, and 4 afterwards,' said the report. '700 police officers were on duty for the game and Superintendent Alan Preston, in charge of the operational control room at Villa Park, said, "It is certainly the biggest soccer crowd operation of its kind ever staged in the West Midlands."'

Even after all of this activity, the weekend was not to finish quietly for us. The next day, a Sunday, Birmingham played West Bromwich Albion at St Andrew's. As home supporters were being escorted into the city centre after the match, a number of them broke away in Jennings Road and ran through the grounds of Aston University. They smashed windows and damaged a JCB excavator parked on the site. We assessed video footage from cameras in the university grounds but there was nothing pursuable, unfortunately, and our covert men had had to stay in the escort. Evidence later emerged that a fight had been arranged outside St Andrew's between West Bromwich Albion fans and Zulus. A sizeable home mob turned up but no Albion, and no opposition meant no fight.

*

The following Friday – Good Friday, in fact – we deployed covert and overt officers to cover The Crown pub, where we expected a gathering for a Bank Holiday drink. The idea was to get the undercover officers seen more and accepted as regulars. The day passed off uneventfully. We monitored the Hill Street area again the next day, as Birmingham were playing Plymouth Argyle. I liaised with the local sergeant engaged on football intelligence duties but there was nothing of consequence to report. On Bank Holiday Monday, we monitored the away game with Reading, which again passed off peacefully. We were coming to understand which fixtures would attract trouble and those where it simply wasn't going to happen. The next day I had a meeting with the detective inspector who had run the retrospective investigation into the Leeds United riot at St Andrew's in 1985. It gave me a good feel for the way in which visual evidence could be used, as well as an understanding of the nature of the evidence available for the events of that day.

On Saturday, 25 April, we went to the Leeds United versus Birmingham game and received good support from West Yorkshire Police, who corralled the Birmingham supporters after the game through side streets to the railway station, about three miles away from the Elland Road stadium. We had undercover officers out that day as well as the two full-uniform overt spotters. Video taken by the local police at one stage showed two of our undercover officers standing just feet away from their two spotter colleagues and with absolutely no eye contact between them. I myself walked parallel to the 'snake' escort in those unfamiliar streets of Leeds and feeling acutely aware that I was not on home territory.

ALEX: The night before, I was really worried about this game. There was a lot of history between Birmingham and Leeds and I didn't know what we were going to face. As it happened it was a non-event and Birmingham were completely policed out of it. We went by train and it was full of drunks bragging. In the ground there were constant chants of 'Leeds Weeds' from the Birmingham fans to the opposition.

Two of those fans on the football special train, though, were seen by undercover officers opening train carriage doors as it was travelling at speeds of more than fifty miles per hour.

On Saturday, 2 May, we again covered St Andrew's and The Crown for the home game with Grimsby Town, and the following Tuesday we went to a night game at Blackburn Rovers. The latter was another northern venue and another laborious ride home in the dark for us in our unmarked police car, but for the covert officers it served to give them credibility in being seen at away games, especially midweek ones. These evening trips meant long, dull car journeys and very late finishes, when I usually just fell into bed. The house would be in total darkness and silent; no greetings at that time of the day. I have always found something depressing about miles of empty motorway but it did at least give us the chance to talk tactics and tell war stories on the way back. We never expected much from the evening games because they were not attractive for the hardened hooligans and getting to some of these places was quite challenging, especially if they travelled by train. Nonetheless I took the view that we needed to go to get the undercovers out there and seen.

Finally came the last league game of the 1986–87 season: City at home to Shrewsbury Town. In The Crown before the match, covert officers overheard discussions between main Zulus about sending spotters out looking for Shrewsbury followers, and after the game the B Team were running around the city centre looking for away fans, which we deemed to be no coincidence. Some of our usual suspects were seen: B Teamers Sharp, Dek, Benetton, Goofy and Mop, plus Bruno.

It was our last fixture for some weeks, giving us time to figuratively catch our breath and to make plans for the new season due to start in August. Some were able to squeeze in some holiday leave but even if I was away I was always restless until I had put a call in to the office. It was a habit and although I trusted the team to get on with research and case building, I couldn't let go of the job completely. It was a bit like having a daily fix, I imagine, but not so damaging to your health.

Quiet as it was that day, May 9 turned out to be significant for us owing to the keen eyes and ears of two of the undercovers in The Crown. They listened in on a conversation between a number of our main targets, one of whom was openly bragging about the attack on Portsmouth fans at The Fox pub on March 21. 'We really did them,' he bragged. 'They weren't expecting it.' This was where a Zulu charge had been led by an Asian-looking youth wielding a blade. Our targets took great pleasure in relating their version of events, revelling in the accounts of violence of a couple of months before. It's interesting that by simply referring to victims as

'Portsmouth' they were de-personalising the injuries and trauma they had inflicted on opposing fans, some of whom would have been entirely innocent. This is a mindset that I have seen repeatedly over the years whereby the hooligans seek to justify their actions by implying that the violence is limited to consenting adults and willing participants and that little of it is actually personal. This could not be further from the truth and fails to recognise the fear that the yobs inflict on society as a whole, and particularly those members of the public who get caught up in these incidents. Apologies were scarce among football hooligans.

We were never able to positively identify the possibly Asian youth with the knife but believed him to be number 9 on our list, nicknamed Red. It was definitely him bragging about the incident. A twenty-one-year-old, mixed-race target would subsequently plead guilty to affray over that incident and be jailed for six months, with a consecutive twenty-one months for admitting an unrelated offence of Section 20 wounding. Another twenty-year-old ('Rooky') from Castle Bromwich later pleaded guilty to unlawful assembly at The Fox and violent disorder in the Hill Street incident and got a twelve-month suspended prison sentence. He would though plead not guilty to delivering a noxious substance, namely Olbas oil, with intent to disable people in The Fox. Nine other people were to be charged with unlawful assembly and affray in respect of this incident as a result of the evidence gathered, including some of our main targets.

*

On 23 May, Scotland played England in an international fixture at Hampden Park in Glasgow. Off the field of play it would be described as a day of mayhem, with over 237 arrests. More than 6,000 English fans journeyed north and of those arrested, a fair few came from the Midlands and were found to have Zulu Warrior calling cards on them. That might explain why our covering The Crown on the same day proved uneventful.

Although we had little evidence proving a connection, other incidents around that time certainly bolstered our suspicions that certain activities, attitudes and habits were influenced by the Zulus. One such incident was an attack by a large mob of youths on the police in the E Division of the city, in Stechford, a fertile recruiting ground for the gang. Under the headline 'Funfair Mob in Attack on PC' the Birmingham Sunday Mercury reported: 'A policeman narrowly escaped being blinded when he was hit by a brick thrown at him as he faced a mob outside a funfair in Birmingham. Police ordered the fair to shut to avoid copycat rioting. PC Stephen Anderson was first on the scene when violence erupted outside Bob Wilson's Fun Fair in Stechford Lane, Stechford. A gang of about 150 youths had gathered and a wine shop was being stoned. As he faced the rampaging mob, PC Anderson was struck in the face with a brick, badly gashing his cheek just below his left eye. He was taken to East Birmingham Hospital where stitches were inserted.' The officer was lucky not to have been blinded, and after he was felled the rioting continued for forty-five minutes, during which the window of a panda car was smashed. It took twenty officers to restore order and two youths were arrested for disorderly conduct.

It was also around that time that the Labour Party's deputy leader, Roy Hattersley, was lucky to escape unhurt when he and some constituency colleagues were attacked by Tottenham Hotspur supporters in a Birmingham hotel. The yobs threw plates at them, and Sir Stanley Yapp, the Birmingham Sparkbrook constituency party chairman, was taken to the Accident Hospital with severe cuts to his face. Coachloads of Spurs supporters had arrived at the hotel, entered the dining room and hurled the plates at Mr Hattersley and his friends, while apparently singing obscene songs and chanting, 'Tax cuts, tax cuts.' They had registered at the hotel as a 'Bankers and Brokers Party of London'!

This spreading of hooligan-type disorder to venues outside football continued when England played Pakistan in a one-day international at Warwickshire County Cricket's Edgbaston ground, in Birmingham, on Monday, 25 May. Drunken fans repeatedly invaded the pitch and fights broke out on the terracing. Police intelligence suggested that a number of drunken, white Zulu Warriors were involved, despite the supposed racial neutrality of the gang. WPC Theresa Sharples, who was on duty at the ground, saved the life of twenty-four-year-old Riaz Mohammed by administering first aid to him. In a truly shocking incident, he needed ten stitches to repair his severed jugular vein and windpipe after being struck by flying glass while watching the match. There had been a scuffle in the crowd in front of him, at which point he had stood up to see what was happening. Almost immediately he was struck by a missile in the neck. It came from a group of mixed white and Asian men who were standing behind him and was believed to have been thrown by a white male aged about twenty-five years.

There was inevitable press speculation as to whether the 'English Disease' of hooliganism, normally associated with football only, would now spread to international cricket but our belief was that this was alcohol-fuelled yobbery at its most basic and not solely a soccer issue. I believed we would be proven right. The day after the events at the cricket match, Sports Minister Dick Tracey said that the Government would consider increasing police strength at cricket matches to control crowds. He feared that the violence could be the start of a new development in sports 'troubles'. In my view, his suspicions were understandable if not entirely realistic. The Home Secretary, Douglas Hurd, also called for an urgent report on the violence and said that he might consider extending the ban on drink at soccer matches to cricket grounds.

Many reports in the media then appeared, regarding the possibility of Birmingham council officers insisting on football stadium-type barriers being installed to separate rival fans at Edgbaston cricket ground, to prevent any more crowd violence. The warning was given in a report to the city's planning committee. The capacity at the cricket ground was 17,450. The report, by John Hales, said: 'Officers involved in administering legislation covering the safety of sports grounds have been concerned that the unruly behaviour and hooligan element experienced at football matches in recent years has begun to show in the behaviour of crowds attending one-day cricket games. This trend is likely to

increase while the incidence of hooliganism in society generally continues to grow.' Again, the view was not necessarily
shared by us.

CHAPTER 8

THE CROWN CONFRONTATION

A T THE END of May, I briefed the team on the progress and overall strategy of Operation Red Card. My general view was that all of it had so far been 'satisfactory'; I certainly had no complaints about the team's efforts. Our work for the season was not yet over, however. That night, a Friday, I set four of the undercover officers the task of visiting The Crown as part of their integration into the premises and so they would be seen as part of the regular football clientele.

By coincidence, the Division Two play-off final between Leeds United and Charlton Athletic was being replayed that afternoon – the first two games had resulted in a draw – and St Andrew's had been chosen as a neutral venue. The occasion demanded a large policing operation in the city centre and at the ground and West Midlands Police drew up emergency plans for a major exercise. Assistant Chief Constable Paul Leopold had announced that about 300 police officers, some mounted and many with dogs, would be present. Efforts to move the match to a Sunday morning had ultimately come to nothing. No tickets would be on sale to Birmingham City fans, while Leeds had been allocated 13,000 tickets and Charlton

5,000. 'We are anxious that the West Midlands ratepayers will not foot the bill for our operation,' said ACC Leopold. 'It is being forced on us by the reputation of one of the clubs and the crucial nature of the match.'

Perhaps inevitably, large groups of Zulu Warriors prowled the streets looking for Leeds fans to get at, and around thirty people were arrested. Three pubs had problems after the game as Leeds fans attempted to have a drink in Birmingham before their journey home, only to be confronted by locals. A Leeds fan of Asian descent was stabbed in the hand while a van was wrecked though this was not directly attributable to Zulus. The following report appeared in the local press soon after:

A gang of soccer thugs mugged a disabled soccer fan for his England football shirt – and left him on the brink of death in a Birmingham street. Thirty-year-old Ian Hartley spent a week in Smethwick's Midland Centre for Neurosurgery after he was found semi-naked and unconscious on the pavement with a fractured skull and severe facial injuries. After seven days he was deemed to be stable and out of danger at which point detectives were allowed to interview him for the first time. Mr Hartley, from Leeds, told police that he was in Birmingham to see the promotion clash between Leeds United and Charlton Athletic at St Andrew's. After the game he went for a drink at the nearby Sampson & Lion pub on the corner of Yardley Green Road and Blakeland Street, Small Heath, but left when the talk turned to football and the atmosphere became tense. A police spokesman said, 'The last thing he remembers is walking up the street, looking over his shoulder and seeing a group of men marching after him with pool cues in their hands. Partly disabled after a fall some years previous he was unable to get away from his attackers.'

Despite all of this, we'd had no specific intelligence suggesting that the local hooligans would be out in force or had anything sinister planned at The Crown that night, and nothing to confirm that any of our targets would even be present. Our officers' trip to the pub was purely to help build their 'legends'. Along with giving strict instructions to keep their alcohol consumption low, I had told the undercover men to swig their beer from bottles, as it is then difficult for others to see how much alcohol they are actually drinking. Police officers in drink cannot make reliable witnesses, and while they worked in their covert roles they had to keep alert and never let their guard down.

That evening I set up the first floor office as the Hill Street observations point again, with Mark and Liam, the two officers normally employed overtly as spotters. Both were wholly committed, strong-minded and fearless when out on the streets in uniform. Again a warning signal of baseball cap being placed on head was the plan in case of any trouble, though an obvious snag was that the camera team had no way of seeing into the pub's interior.

A wooden sign next to the entrance to The Crown advertised the pub's nightly Happy Hour. The next hour certainly would not be one such time. As we hidden officers watched our six covert colleagues enter the pub separately in pairs – Colin and Adam, Don and Reece, and finally Alex and

Danny – we then had to wait for what probably felt much longer than the actual duration. And their numbers were soon reduced:

COLIN: All six of us were in The Crown to start with but Mike had asked us to cover New Street Station for the end of the game between Charlton and Leeds, so we left early and left the other four in there. When we got to the station it was dead quiet and we couldn't understand why. Then we found out it had gone to extra time. We wandered back to The Crown just as the doors were opened and we saw Alex and Danny. They looked in shock and it was obvious that something at happened. We went back into The Crown but the atmosphere was tense and we had one drink and left.

ALEX: We were sat at one of the tables in the main room. I was with my partner and [target] Bruno and the other two under-covers were sitting at another table close by. The place was full and some of the older Birmingham element were there, including an old fat guy we nicknamed Fossil, target 36, and another with a ginger beard who we called, not very crea-tively, Ginger Beard, target 43, and a big guy with white hair. It was like it was all orchestrated because the outside doors were kept deliberately closed while the two doormen came inside the room, and the bar staff stopped serving. The big, white-haired guy was called Kevin and he came over to us, pointed to the five of us one by one and said 'You are Old Bill' to each of us in turn. He took the lead throughout and we were surrounded by over a dozen of them.

They started questioning us in a childish and amateurish way about how many supporters had gone to what match and what the chants were. The 'Leeds Weeds' one came up as a question. We were feeling pretty vulnerable and I started to try and work out how I could throw a bar stool through the window to get attention outside. We stood up and fronted them and offered them outside. At least that way we would have been seen from the observations point over the road. Bruno chipped in and said, 'They're not Old Bill, we go everywhere together.' To some extent he saved us a bit. They all started bickering amongst themselves and didn't know who to believe. We stood our ground and it got to the point where they weren't sure, so they got deflated. A lot left and I went straight to the bar for a drink. I tried to talk to the guy with the white hair but he was having none of it and he blanked me. He had obviously made his mind up.

We left with Bruno and started wandering around the city centre. We saw some Villa fans and finished up on New Street Station where Bruno confronted some British Transport Police and got arrested for being drunk and disorderly. We legged it and made our way back to the nick. The debrief was intense and emotions were running high but our evidence still needed to be recorded. We weren't going anywhere until it was done.

COLIN: The day after the confrontation, Mike asked me and Adam to go back into The Crown to see what was going on. At that point it was us or nobody. We didn't want to go in and I was nervous as hell but we went for it, not before a couple of drinks for Dutch courage. It was a Saturday lunchtime and it was packed. People were talking about what had happened the night before and it was pretty scary.

ADAM: The Crown helped us to develop our tradecraft. After the confrontation we said that if we had trouble we would probably vault the bar and try to barricade ourselves in somewhere at the back until help came. The bar was a curved shape and we used to stand by the curved bit so we knew that we wouldn't be able to get to the door. The main Zulus used to stand in the corner the furthest from the door. There were tables there and Francis used to sit there surrounded by the others. It was difficult to listen.

From our observation point in the opposite building, as soon as we saw our four undercovers leaving The Crown we realised that something had gone wrong: they looked worried and wary. We met up back at the incident room later. Understandably, they were badly shaken by the events in the pub. It transpired that they had been chatting to one of our targets, Bruno, when they were confronted by up to fifteen unknown white men brandishing pool cues and pint glasses, accusing all five of them of being police officers. Bruno, the tall, athletic and well-built lad who could look after himself in a fight, was a big factor in their coming out of the situation unscathed. He had been incensed at the accusation of being a police officer and made no secret of this to his accusers, who eventually backed off in an uneasy truce after a twenty-minute grilling. The undercover officers also stood their ground and had counter-attacked those making the accusations.

Unsurprisingly, our officers' morale hit a low because of this whole drama and as a result I had some serious thinking to do to improve matters. I decided to take the drastic step of giving all four officers involved the option of withdrawing from Operation Red Card, promising them there would be no negative repercussions or criticism. As a result of this offer, two of them, Don and Danny, did decide to leave. I didn't try to influence them either way. Continuing to involve a person who felt he was working under unreasonable duress would not work out and could well cause damage to the operation further down the line. They left with the dignity of knowing that they had done a good job, and I had every respect for the courage that they had shown in facing their fears and coming to a difficult decision. We were in a profession where showing your true feelings was not always the done thing and it would have been easy for them to carry on but without any genuine desire to really make an impact. After both had taken time out to come to terms with their decision, they left the operation officially on 1 July. I had then to make sure that they were not deployed in uniform anywhere close while the operation was in progress. They could not be seen in police uniform until we had finished our work, as they could easily have been recognised and Red Card would have collapsed simply by association.

Of course, none of this was a time for celebration and it wasn't helped by my handling of the 'Bruno situation': because of his significant support during the confrontation, there was a degree of Stockholm syndrome, or sympathy, from my officers towards him. I had to make it clear that he would be having his day in court along with all the other criminals. It was not a popular decision but it had to be remembered that he had only inadvertently protected them; he certainly was not aware that they were police officers. Had he been, we would have been looking at a much more serious scenario, I was convinced of that. He would later receive just a fine for affray, so perhaps a satisfying balance of justice was achieved after all.

Danny had been one of the two officers at the Hill Street incident, and up to that point had fitted into his role with ease, even adding some ear piercing and blond highlights to his hair. He was a Jack-the-lad type who mixed well and on the face of it was very confident. The second officer who left, Don, was an experienced surveillance operative, very clean-cut with short, black hair, personable and generally relaxed but with a propensity to smoke too much, and a cheeky grin which belied his serious nature. He was a methodical individual who liked to be given clear direction. I believe that after the confrontation he simply weighed up the odds and came to the logical conclusion that he did not want to risk putting himself in the same situation again. I was disappointed with their decision but not with them, in fact I couldn't really blame them at all. I suppose one could say that we had been fortunate that none of the undercover officers had been exposed or sussed. The events were a stark reminder too that the remaining officers needed to be permanently on their guard.

On one occasion before The Crown drama, a target had asked one of the undercover officers for his telephone number. Under pressure, our man gave the target a false number. It came out later in one of our debrief sessions, and we knew we would have to address it otherwise the target might become suspicious. So the next time the target was seen, the same undercover officer raised the subject himself and 'owned up', saying that he had given a wrong number because he was wanted by the police and he needed to be careful to avoid arrest. This officer was in fact one of the two who left after the confrontation took place, and when he did we made sure another undercover officer told the target that he had been arrested and was now serving a prison sentence. Fortunately the target believed the story and so their cover remained intact.

As a reaction to the departure of the covert officers, I decided to take a risk and put the two remaining undercover officers together. It was a good move, as Alex and Reece bonded almost like brothers and would continue to play major roles in the inquiry. Alex was the shorter of the two, an intense individual who you could always read from his eyebrows. If one of his brows became raised it meant he was unhappy about something, and if they both became raised it was time to worry! He was absolutely fearless but also had a very sensitive side to his character which made him really likeable. An Aston Villa supporter, he had been at the forefront of the Hill Street incident and was the calming influence in both of the partnerships he worked in. He was absolutely determined to finish the job and I was equally determined to keep him with us. He was a quality officer, if at times a little argumentative. They grew stronger from the experience although for some unknown reason, from that day onwards, Reece insisted on having a skinhead haircut every week without fail. He had an infectious sense of humour and would laugh loudly at the slightest of jokes, usually his own, which was slightly irritating but helped lighten the mood even at very stressful times. If anything this officer was the one who most immersed himself in the covert role and would take the longest to reintegrate into normal policing as a result. He never hesitated to get up close to targets. You could not help but like him and I kept him with me during the file preparation stage to give him more time to settle back into normality, whatever normality was.

It took a few weeks to negotiate with senior officers the recruitment of two replacements and frustratingly I wasn't able to get the pair integrated into the team until August, which would be just in time for the start of the new football season. It had been a difficult time but failure was not something I ever contemplated, I knew that we just had to keep going with what resources we had. One of the new men, James, from my old force the British Transport Police, was a serious-minded, level-headed individual with strong family values. He once told me that his uncle had also been a BTP officer in the 1960s and claimed to be the detective constable responsible for writing the original crime report for the Great Train Robbery. I knew I could rely on James implicitly. To complicate matters however, like Alex he was an avid Aston Villa fan, which would make a convincing disguise as a Blue that little bit harder. With a mass of curly brown hair, and often dressed in either an Adidas top with '77' on or a brown crew neck woollen jumper with an ugly pattern, he was never going to be a fashion icon. He had completed two stints on a British Transport Police public order unit based in the West Midlands and so had broad experience and a good feel for football gang culture. That experience, though, meant there was a higher risk of him being identified as a policeman. To his great credit, it was a risk he was prepared to take.

James's new working partner would be Lee, who came from a surveillance background on my division. They had never previously met. On first appearances, Lee probably looked like a big beer drinker but he wasn't at all. None of the coverts could really be described as smartly dressed but Lee was definitely the scruffiest of the bunch. He would wear an un-ironed white T-shirt tucked into his jeans which made a not insubstantial belly look even larger, with a tatty, grey, zip-up jumper over the top. His nickname of 'Dog Breath' was hardly a compliment but he wasn't at all uncomfortable with it and in fact, odd as it seems, he seemed to revel in the infamy. My recollection is that all officers on the Divisional Observations Teams had nicknames as well as radio call signs so that when they were speaking to each other by radio it was harder to identify them if anyone was surreptitiously listening in on that channel. Lee's tired-looking eyes always gave the impression he was sleep-deprived but those features hid a lively if mildly eccentric intelligence and a useful ability to operate calmly under pressure. He was also keen: in his own words, 'Mike asked me if I wanted to do it and I jumped at the chance and said yes. That was it.'

JAMES: In July 1987 I was approached by West Midlands Police to join a covert operation regarding Birmingham City supporters. I joined a team of undercover officers. I had no training but changed my appearance. I went with my new partner to the old Bull Ring and in one jewellery shop had a gold stud in my left ear. He paid for it and it hurt! I grew my hair and had it gelled back and grew a scruffy beard. My partner had near shoulder length hair and a huge beard. His nickname was Dog Breath – the shame. My part was to get close to Birmingham supporters that travelled on the rail network, and we were all under instructions not to get involved in any violence. I had an alias name of James Foster, employed as a window cleaner, and had a Birmingham City membership card, which gave access to the Main Stand, Block B. This was particularly hard as I am a Villa fan. The irony was that on the back of the card, the fourth condition of membership stated that 'The holder's membership shall be terminated if the holder fails to maintain a good standard of behaviour before, during and after the match.' I obviously had to learn all about Birmingham City, which was also very painful! On one of my days off I went shopping with my wife and met an old friend who knew I was a police officer. He looked at me and said, 'You look a bit rough, you look like one of those football hooligans.' We both laughed when he had gone.

Neither James nor Lee really fitted the image of young, hardcore Zulus but we were at the stage of the inquiry – with less than two months remaining – where we already had some excellent evidence, so I wasn't overly troubled by this. The priority was that they stayed safe while doing the best they could to help us put the icing on the cake, so to speak, when it reached prosecution stages.

> **LEE:** The biggest thing that pissed me off was that I used to go into The Crown and start playing the one-armed bandit. You never looked around, I always had my back deliberately to them. I put five quid in the machine one day and got nothing from it. Adam came in and put one coin in and got the jackpot. I couldn't say anything to him but I looked at him out of the corner of my eye and thought, you fucker. For some reason I always had a feeling that one of the barmaids was on to us and there was another regular in there that I always felt uneasy about.

I took a few photographs of seven out of the eight undercover officers when we were in the safety of our office premises. It wasn't intended to be anything formal, just a few light-hearted group shots with plenty of grins and arm-waving going on. For a few moments they appeared to be more like a bunch of boisterous youngsters but beneath the jovial exterior they all knew how deeply serious this business was. In essence we were operating in a cocoon away from the reality of everyday policing and in a way which was very alien to them. Trying to get into the mindset of a hooligan whilst maintaining the discipline of a police officer was difficult and while these moments of fun and banter were good for morale, I also needed to keep a tight rein. It was not always easy and was frankly sometimes quite a lonely existence, which went with my role. Whilst I kept my senior officers up to date with what was going on at every stage, I also deliberately tried to make as many decisions as I could myself so that we could move on quickly and avoid bureaucracy.

In June, I spent three days with our Chief Inspector (Operations) at Surrey Police HQ, in Guildford, for a National Football Intelligence Conference. We listened to the talks with great interest but were conscious that we still were outside the 'police football family' where each club football intelligence officer had a unique and sometimes fanatical attachment to his own soccer team. These officers protected their roles with a passion that was not always evident in other walks of policing. It was beyond doubt that some of them had an intimate knowledge of their hooligans. Some had less knowledge but liked the freedom that went with the job and the opportunity to visit other parts of the UK. For the chosen few there was even the chance to travel abroad for international games. Once you got onto that circuit you generally became a regular feature of a very 'elite' group.

At about that time, the Home Secretary, Douglas Hurd, claimed that the police were 'winning the battle to combat football hooliganism' and that crowds were returning to matches – with the glaring exception of Birmingham City. 'Closed circuit television and controls on alcohol have been key weapons in the crackdown which has seen crowds increase at most West Midlands soccer grounds,' reported one newspaper. 'Only Birmingham City showed a drop in attendances last season. Mr Hurd outlined existing and proposed new measures and highlighted a dramatic increase in arrests. A total of 2,008 arrests were made at First Division games with 3,532 ejected and 1,708 arrested at Second Division games with 1,255 persons ejected. West Midlands Police arrested 681 fans in or near the six league clubs in the County. Birmingham City's average attendance dropped to 7,423 from 10,805.'

We knew we still had much to do.

*

The new season began for us on Saturday, 15 August, with Birmingham City at home to Stoke City, another club with a substantial and highly active hooligan following. Scores of Birmingham supporters, Zulu Warriors amongst them, congregated at the 49ers bar in St Martin's Circus to drink, to play pool and to plan tactics and militaristic manoeuvres. The bar was directly opposite the main access to New Street Station and most there were waiting for away supporters arriving by rail.

At 1.50 p.m., around sixty Stoke fans emerged from the railway station. A similar portion of the Birmingham contingent left the 49ers bar to track them. The inevitable confrontation took place in Manzoni Gardens, an open-space pedestrianised area between the station and the Bull Ring Shopping Centre. Despite being almost surrounded by busy roads, Manzoni Gardens had once been renowned as a pleasant place to stroll around or just sit and relax. Latterly it had become notorious for drunks and for anti-social behaviour. On one side were slightly raised flower beds, wooden benches and a wide paved walkway; on the other, a grassed area with public conveniences in a corner where, years before, I made the grisly discovery of a plastic bag containing the body of an unborn child. Today, although there was no vehicular access, twenty on-foot police officers were quickly on the scene, managing to disperse both groups without casualties.

Closer to the 3 p.m. kick-off, more home supporters, including a few B Teamers, were standing outside the Watering Hole pub in Coventry Road, a stone's throw from St Andrew's stadium. Watched by our two new covert officers, James and Lee, and target Bruno, a few of the men did indeed launch stones and other projectiles at Stoke supporters' coaches passing by on their way to the football ground. Several windows were broken and a few fans were cut by glass fragments. Any away supporters walking in the vicinity of the Watering Hole did so at their own risk, with verbal abuse as well as beer glasses often aimed at them from the direction of the pub. The OSU made one arrest a short while after a third Stoke supporters' coach had been targeted.

LEE: We were at the Watering Hole. It was a bright sunny day. People were picking up stones beforehand to throw at the Stoke coaches. In fact there were even stones put to one side inside the pub. As Stoke went past they just let fly. After the game, in Great Barr Street, I saw them smashing the windows of a factory. The OSU were trying to get control and all the time the Zulu chants were going.

Birmingham City went on to win the game 2–0 and there was a buoyant mood amongst their supporters. Nevertheless, after the game a large number of them were being escorted by the police in Lawley Street and Curzon Street, towards the city centre, when a few splintered off and burst through the police lines to charge at nearby Stoke fans. It was a good example of how separate groups suddenly merged under the banner of the Zulu Warriors.

COLIN: I was with Adam when the mounted officers were charging at us. I saw two officers grab one youth by the shoulders one either side as they rode by. He shot forward and didn't stop running. There was loads of baton charges and fighting everywhere.

ADAM: We were inside the ground. We came out with the main body of the fans, in a group of a couple of hundred. We started to hear that they had organised a knock. We went up a road from the park by Watery Lane. We were running with them just off the front about fifteen people back. We turned into a sort of terraced road and about halfway down there were at least five police horses stationary. Everyone came to a stop, not quite knowing what to do. I then saw a third of a house brick come flying over my head and just bounce off the tarmac and sort of roll and end up just at the feet of one of the horses. The PC riding it looked down and looked dismissive. The mounted officers then all drew their long batons with a sweeping movement from left to right and spurred their horses into a walk. As they started to walk they were so close to each other you couldn't get between them.

Everyone started to turn and started to run back a couple of hundred yards towards the park. The police horses were then spurred into a trot. Everyone made a right turn. Bearing in mind we were now at the back and tightly packed in, we started to worry. As I looked back, the horses went into a canter. You could see the ears of the horses pinned back. They were filling the road. We were sprinting by now and we went right with the crowd. I looked around again and one horse was at full gallop, digging up tarmac in the road with his hooves. They all started galloping and were starting to catch up with people who were either knocked over by the horses or 'staffed'. This was proper scary and I was thinking that there was no way of getting away from them.

As we ran from them we then ran into a line of police dog handlers, perhaps five or six. They filled the road. The police had their dogs in their left hands and staffs in their right hands. I thought which side to try and run past and decided to go for the staff side. I just didn't fancy getting bitten. Colin and I were running side by side and managed to get up against a small picket fence. I saw one horse literally push a group of five over the fence and then jump it and start rounding them up in the park. The dog men were engaging with the fans. It was proper, proper scary. Colin and I managed to get away from the group and make off.

Two of Red Card's main Zulu targets, Fats and Midwest, were subsequently charged with violent disorder, along with seven of the B Team: Sharp, Benetton, Dek, Mop, Goofy, Baby Face and Stone, as well as Oburn, who would become better acquainted to us as 'the Diary Man' (and indeed 'the Historian'). Once again our two overt officers made two arrests, under Section 4 of the Public Order Act. The two arrests were Stoke fans though, both of whom were ultimately fined £400 each.

It was normal practice for West Midlands Police to escort away fans from St Andrew's on foot all the way to New Street by means of the slow-moving 'snake' column, trying to cope with potential ambush points in and around the Digbeth area at the same time. The Operational Support Unit, from which I had drawn staff for Red Card, was usually at the forefront. Working in serials of a sergeant and ten constables, and using the force's transit vans, they were immensely experienced in public order situations and extremely effective in dealing with crowd disorder. Any prisoners taken during these deployments would simply be bundled into the accompanying vans, which were usually crowded by the time they reached the city centre. They were tightly knit teams and if one officer entered the fray to arrest anyone then the others followed, regardless of how many people opposed them. Officers always moved forwards, never backwards. Notably too, in those days the units were very much the preserve of men. It seems that the Zulus were not the only ones not readily accepting women into their ranks.

The finale would usually take place on the concourse at New Street Station as away fans sought to get trains home while home fans tried to give them a leaving present. Any time after 5.15 p.m. on a Saturday was usually not a good time to be a normal railway passenger.

LIAM: It kicked off massive after the Stoke match. It was basically lock someone up, throw them in the back of a van to deal with later and get back out for the next. I had a couple of prisoners. It was massive, with truncheons out. Stoke gave the Blues a good fight all the way from the traffic island at Watery Lane all the way up into the city centre. Blues were coming at us constantly from all the side streets and a fat West Indian I knew well got arrested. It was like the knock from hell, the Zulus knew the route we took the away supporters back to the city centre and would wait to ambush us. Just before Red Card I was involved in another big fight in the same location but this time it was Nottingham Forest. It was like a routine.

Later that month we were unfortunate enough to attend both legs of City's Littlewoods Cup tie against Mansfield Town. The first leg was a 2–2 draw away in Nottinghamshire and in the return at St Andrew's City lost 1–0. There were no incidents of note to report and all of this exposure to football left me hating the game even more!

On Tuesday, 1 September, Birmingham had a night game in south-east London against Millwall, a club with one of the most notorious followings in football. This was regarded as a high-risk game and West Midlands Police worked closely with the Metropolitan Police for the occasion. Thankfully the night passed off without great incident, probably because evening kick-offs and long midweek journeys were not really attractive propositions to the Zulu Warriors, even against hated rivals like these. For those with jobs, be they hooligans or just normal fans, midweek away trips could be problematic enough without annoying their employers by taking time off for long football journeys or returning late. The lack of late-night return trains from London to Birmingham was another deterrent.

Although the two new undercover officers went to the game, on a supporters' coach, I was not expecting a great deal from the fixture in terms of evidence gathering but had thought it worth a try anyway.

> COLIN: You change from being a uniform police officer to being something that you are not and so you feel different. I had a discussion with Mike Layton about going on a coach. I knew that Mike was focused on what he was trying to achieve but sometimes I used to think, it's not worth the risk. I just didn't want to go to Millwall that day. I thought it was too risky and that we would be too isolated. He didn't make me and Adam go but some of the others did go.

This was a difficult one because I knew that on the one hand Colin was right but he couldn't be seen to be just opting out and getting his own way. It was about none of us losing collective face and I had to handle it delicately. I didn't like it but I needed not to make a big deal out of it either. I made it clear that on this occasion we could manage without them going. They were not needed.

Millwall's home was The Den in Cold Blow Lane, a quite appropriate name, a notorious place distinctly lacking in warmth or welcome. The pair got to The Den safely but as the local police would not allow them access to local pubs and the like, the visiting fans were forced to stand on the away end terraces and just wait for kick-off on the bare terraces of a decrepit old stadium which held scant appeal and very few comforts.

LEE: Me and James went to Millwall by coach. I think it was Prospect Coaches. There was another coach with some of the hooligan element on who disappeared off towards East London once there was no police escort. It was like going into a bear pit. No arguing with the police about searches when you went in to the ground; you were searched or stuffed against a wall by the throat. The atmosphere was one of just waiting for it to happen: totally intimidating, with lines of police.

To make matters grimmer for the travelling supporters, the away end was set behind twelve-foot-high fences topped with spikes. Millwall went on to beat Birmingham 3–1, making a miserable night even worse for the Midlanders, who just wanted to get home as quickly as possible. Speedy departures from there were uncommon though, owing to the numbers of Millwall yobs wanting to bid their own brand of fond farewell to visitors. As the Birmingham fans' coach was leaving the car park, a brick smashed through one of the side windows just in front of where the undercover officers were seated. The attack caused much agitation amongst the Brummies but the Metropolitan Police escort waved the coach driver to just keep going out of the area. It made for a few tense moments and a very draughty journey back to Birmingham as the wind blew through the hole in the broken window. There was not much to sing about: just mile after mile of black tarmac motorway.

CHAPTER 9

DEADLY RIVALS

SATURDAY, 22 AUGUST 1987 was a typical British summer's day: cool and rainy. It was also a red letter day for Operation Red Card. My officers would obtain valuable conspiracy evidence against eleven targets involved in violence when Birmingham City played Aston Villa in a local derby – the local derby – at Villa Park. Our cameras were again in use in the office overlooking The Crown pub and we also obtained video evidence from the mobile Hoolivan camera. Still photographs were taken too, showing some of our main targets on the terraces, something of a rare event.

Many Blues fans gathered in the city centre pubs close to New Street Station, in particular The Crown and The Grapes in Hill Street, both of which were already full by eleven o'clock in the morning. Our two new undercover officers, James and Lee, deployed to The Grapes, had to endure a very nervy few moments. James, the British Transport Police officer, looked across the bar and straight into the face of a Birmingham hooligan called Dean, who knew him as a policeman. Fortunately for us, Dean was so drunk that after what felt like an age for James he turned around and continued talking with his mates, having not recognised him. The two officers left in haste.

By two o'clock, all of the Birmingham fans had left the pubs to go to New Street Station, where the same two officers joined a train to Witton, the nearest station to Villa Park. Well over three hundred boisterous supporters crammed into the carriages. During the ten-minute journey to Witton, they smashed the interior lighting, tore down ceiling panels and slashed seat covers with blades. The doors on trains had individual locking mechanisms and one of our targets, a white nineteen-year-old from Yardley Wood who we named 'Comedian' (target 56), was seen opening doors as the train reached a speed of sixty miles per hour. He was later charged with endangering the safety of passengers.

On arrival at Witton, the hyped-up horde of Blues burst out of the carriages, singing their favourite song, 'Shit on the Villa', with gusto. The acrimony between these two sets of hooligans was often extreme, and the local derbies always had potential flashpoints throughout the entire day. These short rail journeys were constantly problematic for the BTP owing to the high volume of people and the frequency of the local trains. With a relatively small number of staff anyway, they could not patrol everywhere and so had to be experts in risk management, which in the most trying circumstances had to be precise. The hooligans knew that even with a police escort on the train, they could often get away with a lot of destructive behaviour. At worst, you might have just two officers on a train filled with hundreds of supporters; at best, you might have seven. In that situation, while you would always try to keep a 'sterile' space between you and the hooligans, it was not always possible and you were almost constantly being tested for a response. As a police officer I learnt that when yobs were playing up, a good tactic was to decide on one intended target, focus on the evidence against him rather than trying to watch them all, and then grab him as the train arrived at its destination, when most people were more concerned with getting off it. You would then steer your subject towards officers deployed on static duties at the railway station with as much speed and stealth as you could.

Colin was working covertly in the run-up to the match.

COLIN: We stayed close to a target called Meatloaf during the summer. We went to The Crown on the day of the Villa match in August but couldn't get in. We were queuing at another place around the corner and Meatloaf saw us and took us to the front. He knew the doormen and took us in. He kept introducing us to a load of real nutters. He told us there was an arrest warrant out for him. We went to The Crown with him and stood on the tables chanting, 'Shit on the Villa'. We went on a local train to Witton and there was a lone Villa fan on the train who seemed to have learning difficulties. They literally covered him in spit. I wanted to jump in and stop them. I didn't feel right. It was just a mad day. At the game itself the Zulus got close to the Holte End to get at the Villa fans and were agitating all of the time.

Once inside the football ground, the covert officers went into the old Witton Lane Stand with the away contingent. There they saw Blues supporters ripping seats away from their floor fixings even as their team went on to beat Aston Villa 2–0. Although there was no televisual evidence of the vandalism, black and white photographs were snatched clandestinely. The crowd standing on the terraces included certain Red Card targets, such as Green Hood and Milk Race, but they were not careless or silly enough to be caught on film inside a stadium ripping up seats or vandalising. Francis was also at the game. Video footage showed him at one point move from a seat right at the back of the stand to very close to the Villa fans. In fact he was stopped by a uniform officer from going any further.

The first goal sparked a bit of a pitch invasion and then there was a general movement towards the Villa fans in the Holte End, who also tried to get over the fence at the Blues support. Matters on the pitch were heated too, which was not a surprise given the highly charged occasion, with a crowd of more than 30,000 spectators. More than fifty fouls were committed in the game and players were booked for a variety of transgressions including scuffling, dangerous play and wild tackling. Violent behaviour from the footballers cannot be realistically held up as a reason or justification for violence on the terraces, but it is never helpful for keeping the peace either.

LEE: In Hill Street, around The Crown, you could just feel the atmosphere of impending fighting. There was hundreds milling about. We went to New Street Station by the back entrance. It was clearly organised. On the train we were shoulder to shoulder. The lights were smashed just as we left the platform before even entering the tunnels. Constant singing and chanting and 'Zulu, Zulu' all the time. There were no uniformed police on the train. We were met by the OSU at Witton and herded together. Something had been definitely planned. There was a small pitch invasion on the halfway line with about two dozen Blues fans. Mike [Layton] got pissed off with one of the DCs who was out with a camera that day inside the ground but for some reason didn't take any pictures of them so there was a bit of a lively discussion afterwards.

That damage to the train inflicted by City yobs cost £1,200. I believe that were it not for the heavy rain that day, we would have had more trouble; a good downpour is the best policeman, as they say.

Prime Minister Margaret Thatcher's interest in tackling football violence originally stemmed from a riot at Luton Town involving Millwall fans. This prompted Luton to come up with a membership scheme, so only people on a known database could buy tickets, whilst the Government established a 'war Cabinet' on hooliganism starting with efforts at breaking the perceived, if not necessarily conclusive, link between alcohol and football violence. During 1985 and 1986, ministers met with the football authorities to push forward their agenda relating to CCTV and membership schemes, culminating in Mrs Thatcher meeting the chairman of the FA and the president of the Football League in July 1988 to spell out the message that maintaining the status quo was not an option. National media reports confirmed that the hooligan problem in England was high on Maggie's agenda.

For the Labour Opposition, former Sports Minister Denis Howell backed a 'half and half' plan to keep hooligans out of football matches. He wanted to see a compromise deal between Sports Minister Dick Tracey and the football authorities which would set aside half of each football ground for members only, with the rest open to casual visitors. Mr Howell, the MP for Small Heath in Birmingham, said it 'would be a monstrous interference with civil liberties' to prevent spectators entering grounds unless they had club membership cards and that such restrictions would lead to the death of football. 'I have written to the Home Secretary drawing attention to the totally illogical position of the Government where it says it can do nothing to stop hooligans and evil people going abroad but decent citizens cannot go to see their team playing away in this country,' he added.

Those aforementioned 'nervy moments' were hazards of the job for undercover policemen. We just hoped that the covert officers managed to keep their wits about them. That was not always easy to do, especially during the more intense episodes. Covert partnership Colin and Adam had specific recollections of the target who would become number 40 in our list.

COLIN: Meatloaf was a West Indian in his thirties. He was tall and scruffy and walked with a funny gait. He had terrible body odour. He used to wear a Birmingham City pin badge. Before the Operation I'd arrested him for a public order offence following a game between Birmingham City and Sheffield Wednesday at St Andrew's. After the game he blew a whistle and the Zulus attacked the opposition. We couldn't get to him there and then but we found him on New Street Station and I arrested him for threatening behaviour. There was a violent struggle and we had to fight with him all the way to the van. He was found guilty at court and received a fine.

Around April 1987, when we were on the operation we went into the Toreador Bar in the city centre. Adam and I walked in and Meatloaf was serving behind the bar. He looked at me and I looked at him and I thought 'Shit!' But he only noticed the Blues pin badges we were wearing and started chatting to us. It was amazing, he just had not recognised me. We finished up chatting like best of mates. We visited on a fairly regular basis and he used to tell us about what he had been up to. He told us about the fine and said he had no intention of paying it and that there was a warrant out for him. He also said that he had been involved in a big fight at Stoke. He knew a lot of people working on the doors in the city centre.

ADAM: During the operation we got to know a Blues fan who was a doorman at the Toreador pub near the Markets in Edgbaston Street. He was a black guy into the violence but said that he only went to the games that mattered. We were keen to try and get close to him and chatted to him quite a bit. The weird thing is that Colin had actually arrested him for a football-related public order offence but the guy simply didn't recognise him. One day we were in the pub and four drunks tried to get past the doorman at the door. He stood in the door and started fist fighting with them. They were trying to get him to come out but he stood his ground. We were thinking, shit, this is difficult, will he expect us to help him? We told the licensee that there was some trouble at the door and he grabbed a rounders bat from behind the bar and went out. The four drunks were spitting but they couldn't get the better of the two as they fought between the inner and outer door. They gave up and went off. We were chatting to the doorman and minutes later the Old Bill arrived. By this time the rounders bat was back behind the bar. A police constable said to the licensee, 'We have heard that there has been some trouble.' The licensee said, 'No, nothing here.' The funny thing was that as he was saying this and pouring a pint, blood was trickling down his nose onto his lip from where a blow had landed. The PC just walked out and that was the end of it.

*

The Birmingham Super Prix motor race was held in the city centre that summer, and on Monday, 31 August, licensed houses – pubs, bars and clubs – in the area were permitted to stay open from 10.30 in the morning to 10.30 at night. During the afternoon, Zulu Warriors in small groups gradually entered The Cabin pub at the top of Corporation Street, near to Priory Queensway. This went on until around four o'clock when their numbers had reached twenty-five. At 4.15 p.m., one of them blew a whistle, at which point the Zulus collectively sprang into action, attacking a group of men seated in a corner of the pub, throwing furniture and glasses at them. Six of the victims needed treatment at the General Hospital for various injuries, none of them life-threatening, fortunately. It had been a planned attack by Zulus on Aston Villa followers. Evidence of the violence was obtained from both overt and covert sources resulting in certain Red Card hardcore targets eventually facing charges of violent disorder. Present on this Super Prix Day incident were Francis, Green Hood, Milk Race, Red and Fats.

We later learned, in another report, that it had in fact been a revenge attack: some weeks before, Green Hood had been seen in The Crown by covert officers. He was walking with a stick and sporting two black eyes. He was feeling sorry for himself and was in a 'bit of a state', apparently. The undercover officers overheard him discussing what had happened: he had been attacked by some people in Castle Vale. He was now talking about how to get his own back on his assailants. On the day of the Super Prix the main targets were in town. There was no football for Blues that day but Villa were playing. The group split into twos and threes and entered The Cabin separately. A whistle was blown and about twenty people attacked six people from the Castle Vale area sitting inside. They got 'a good battering'. On the day none of the six would make statements to the police but four subsequently did and three of them were able to identify one of our targets by name.

Conflict between Villa and Blues fans did not just feature at the football matches between the two sides, it extended to other occasions and was well known in the city to be a wider social problem. In other words, it was not strictly a soccer matter and it went back many years. On one infamous occasion, on 31 August 1985, Birmingham had lost at Everton while Villa hosted Luton Town. When Blues fans got back to New Street Station, they heard that Villa were drinking in the Old Contemptibles pub on Newhall Street. Around eighty males bombarded the pub, with roadworks, bottles and a traffic bollard going through the window. Villa came out and skirmishes went on for a few minutes before police arrived, signifying the hostilities ceasing for that day

In early September, we covered Birmingham City's home game with Crystal Palace. Only about fifty away followers turned up by train from London. Our officers followed them down through Digbeth to the football ground without any incidents occurring. On the pitch though, and much to the private pleasure of the Aston Villa fans in our Red Card ranks, Birmingham suffered a humiliating 6–0 defeat. It was a bit of a bad day all round in fact; a home thrashing for the soccer team and no real work or victory achieved for our team.

The following Tuesday, I attended an inspectors' promotion board. I was hoping to climb further up the career ladder. A pre-board report is written on your division with a recommendation to the divisional chief superintendent, in my case Clive Roche, about whether you had the support of your immediate line manager or should not go forward for promotion. Without that support you would not normally advance any further. My report came from Detective Superintendent Roy Taylor. It read: 'He is presently playing a leading part in the running of an Incident Room which is investigating a gang involved in street crime and football hooliganism in the city. He has displayed considerable initiative and qualities of leadership overcoming many problems which other officers of his rank would not attempt, either losing their enthusiasm or folding completely.' Comments were included from Chief Superintendent Clive Roche for my board report (the chief super's board report is read by the interview panel which decides whether you get through or not; the interview was important but the recommendation counted for a lot too). He said of me: 'At present he is a key figure in an operation to deal with organised violence and crime in the city centre associated with gangs of football supporters.'

Whatever the outcome of the interview was to be, I would be told of it in person by Chief Superintendent Roche, as he always got a heads-up before the list of successful candidates was teleprinted and officially confirmed around the force. You just had to wait until a suitable vacancy came up and, if successful, you then went where you were told. I had previously been disappointed at this stage but today I was very pleased to be given the news that I had succeeded in my efforts for promotion. I would have to wait, however; it was nearly a year before I was actually promoted, in August 1988. That wait did not bother me at all because I was happy with what I was doing with Red Card. However, I now had to be very careful indeed not to get a complaint against me or my team, as a promotion would be rescinded if there were any disciplinary issues outstanding and some such investigations took months to complete. So as long as I was leading Red Card, it was a risk for me: any complaints about how the operation was managed would fall on me to a large extent.

The Saturday after my promotion board, we went to City's away game at Swindon Town, liaising on the day with Wiltshire Police. Birmingham won and maybe the good result had a bearing on post-match matters, as there were no crowd incidents to report. However, undercover officer Lee remembers it being a quite worrying afternoon:

> LEE: We were hemmed in at the end of the game to such a point that people started fainting. The police were petrified of the reputation of the Zulus. You became aware of the sections of the crowd that were not remotely interested in what was going on on the pitch.

Reports came in later of unrest before the game involving an estimated six hundred Birmingham fans who had gone to a pub in Swindon. They were refused drinks and so wrecked the pub and smashed its windows. The press also reported a similar incident after the game: 'Police arrested 19 Birmingham City soccer supporters after a fight at a pub in an Oxfordshire village. The fans had stopped at The Crown public house in Woodstock on their way home after watching their team beat Swindon Town 2–0. A Thames Valley Police spokesman said, 'At 11 p.m. a brawl broke out between the fans and some locals. Glasses were smashed and thrown and chairs were also used as weapons but luckily no-one was seriously hurt. But the publican suffered bruising when he was punched in the face as he tried to break up the fighting.' The fans were taken to Banbury Police Station for questioning and later released on police bail.'

On 15 September, we covered the Tuesday evening home game against Blackburn Rovers, which finished in a 1–0 home win, and on 19 September we were at St Andrew's again, and The Crown, for the home game with Shrewsbury Town, a scoreless draw with no 'goals' achieved for us either. We were now approaching the end-date of Operation Red Card, planning for the fixture at Plymouth Argyle, which would also include a trip to Torquay, on Saturday, 26 September. It certainly wasn't a pleasure trip on our part, as it was strongly suspected that violent disorder was top of the Zulus' agenda. Some of our targets had travelled to Torquay and engaged in fighting with some Swansea fans, and Elm had openly bragged about stealing a wallet from one of them. And another twenty-year-old target, from Ward End, subsequently went to prison for twenty-eight days for theft committed in Plymouth and Torquay, and a twenty-seven-year-old from Ladywood got two years' probation for theft. These last two were to become targets 'Ant' and 'Charlie' respectively. They were charged with stealing £100 from a turnstile at the Plymouth ground and jewellery in Torquay.

ANDY MURCOTT: We were expecting some of our targets to go to Torquay when Birmingham City played Plymouth so I was asked to go down on the Friday to stay overnight at a local bed and breakfast. When I got there I liaised with the local CID who told me the landlady had a reputation for being 'up for some fun' but I kept a low profile and my door locked! I spent much of the next day in the CID's cell block monitoring the arrest activity. Some Birmingham fans had come down but not in the numbers we had expected and although there was some trouble it was kept to a minimum and I saw none of the major players.

Definitely in attendance though had been targets Milk Race and Shirt Out, their photographer. In fact, nearly fifty Birmingham fans had travelled by train to Plymouth, and amongst them were the two undercover officers, James and Lee. Plenty of alcohol was swallowed by the Birmingham fans but no bad behaviour was witnessed. Once in Plymouth, they joined up with a hundred and fifty fans already there, effectively taking over a town centre pub before the usual 'show walk' in enemy territory, this time to Argyle's Home Park ground. Football hooligans generally liked to evade the police where possible and when contained by the police, for instance at railway stations, and boxed in to a 'snake' with escorting officers on either side, they often used the opportunity to be as vocal as possible, chanting and singing and generally showing out. The term 'show walk' was coined by James and the message was very much to say, 'We are here, we are strong, we are not frightened of the police, we are not frightened of anyone, we are in your town, and we can take you.' The match finished as a 1–1 draw and afterwards a fight involving up to fifty people took place in the park next to the football ground.

LEE: We went down to Torquay the night before and stayed in a bed and breakfast. James had the whole of the National Rail timetable in his head apart from Saturdays so getting to Plymouth was a bit stressful. After the match Plymouth tried to ambush us in a park and we were not sure how close we were going to be to what was going down but fortunately the police managed to get things under control. Blues had a reputation and just their presence caused chaos with the police.

The two coverts stuck to the script and just observed, not participating or getting too close to any action. They walked back to the station and had an uneventful and long journey back home. This was typical of covert activity where you would have lengthy periods of seeing nothing out of the ordinary, interspersed with intense bursts of evidential activity.

LIAM: There was a big knock at the Plymouth game on the waste ground, a grassed area by the football ground after the match. The local police lost control and were too spread out. Mark and I got in between and confronted them with our truncheons out. It was carnage. The Blues started fighting and Plymouth to be fair had a go back. We were running across the grass trying to break them up. Those were the times when I felt a bit vulnerable; when it started to kick-off we did feel isolated. To some extent we had to be guided by the local police at away games but they did not always take us where we wanted to go, so sometimes we had to take chances. What did help us was that the Zulus knew that we knew who they were and if we were about it did stop some of the trouble.

On Wednesday, 30 September, we covered an evening match with West Bromwich Albion when further evidence was gathered of conspiracy to commit violent disorder in respect of five main targets. Incidentally, Birmingham lost 2–1. Present were targets Francis, Milk Race, Light, Hoop and Midwest.

The last game we covered for Operation Red Card was a home match with Huddersfield Town on Saturday, 3 October, which Birmingham won 2–0. By then we were confident we had what evidence we wanted, so it felt like a bit of an anticlimax. We were ready to finish the job; it was our turn to start putting some scores on the doors. That said, a worrying incident had occurred away from football but reportedly involved hooligan gangs, as covered in the local press on 2 October:

An amateur boxing match at a Birmingham social club ended in a massive crowd brawl. A crowd of thugs wielding knives and machetes ran amok scattering terrified spectators including women and children. Violence flared after the match between the Aston Villa Amateur Boxing Association and Birmingham Irish Club at the Alcan Plate Social Club in Kitts Green. Publican Mr Patrick Flynn, aged 27 years, suffered a serious cut to his right hand when he tried to disarm a man lashing out with a long bladed weapon. Mr Flynn, Vice President of the Birmingham Irish Club, said: 'It had been a brilliant evening until the last bout when I think one fighter was a Villa supporter and the other a Birmingham City fan. Suddenly a gang of coloured men started chanting "Zulu, Zulu" and then ran through the crowd. Punches were thrown and glasses thrown about and all hell broke loose.' He added, 'One big bloke had a machete and he was lashing out at women and young kids.' When police officers arrived just after midnight, the troublemakers had fled.

All of this activity convinced me that we were doing the right thing. It wasn't about just having the right moral compass, it was knowing that things were getting increasingly out of hand. The bloodlust of some of these people was just too much to comprehend. Machetes and children in the same sentence – it had to be stopped.

CHAPTER 10

CLOSING IN

O N THIRTY-NINE specific operational days we had gath-ered evidence against a number of our targets, as well as making twelve arrests which did not prejudice the main Operation Red Card. We had over sixty video cassettes of filmed evidence of criminal activity and association, all of which as a matter of procedure had been viewed, catalogued and cross-referenced in detail. We were ready to go.

On one occasion, help was requested from within the force in relation to certain Red Card targets who were not actually known for public order offences but were believed to be active in other crimes, mainly organised shoplifting. Here I had George, probably the most prolific informant I have ever dealt with. As a result of his information, in July an operation was mounted which resulted in the arrest of two people for burglary at the Midlands Electricity Showroom in Kidderminster, and four arrests for receiving stolen property. Regrettably, my relationship with my informant ended on an unhappy note when sometime later I paid him out for some information and he promptly went out with the money, got drunk and committed a burglary himself. He was arrested.

I met him as he left the police station the following morning after being charged and made my feelings known in no uncertain terms. He had gone off the rails and broken the trust that we had developed. I never saw him again.

A character named 'Woody' had come to our attention, target 20. Although he was not initially suspected of any Zulu activity, which explained why he wasn't at first a target on our list, we learned that he was associated with the gang.

ANDY MURCOTT: Woody was not very high in the hierarchy of the Zulu Warriors and he was not at every event, but he was an active participant. He was one of those who had other criminal interests. He arrived at The Crown licensed house on several occasions in a hire car. We investigated how much he was spending on hire cars and came to the conclusion it was about £600 every month, which was a lot in those days, and he was travelling about 1,000 miles every month. It prompted us to set up a surveillance operation to explore what he was doing. I spent several weeks with the Force Surveillance Unit, initially with the junior team and then with the more experienced team who took on the harder jobs. The junior team followed Woody to several locations within Birmingham but he didn't commit any crime.

On the last occasion, they followed him down towards Bristol on the M5. He was never the driver but took up a position in the back seat and was obviously aware of surveillance methods because he was constantly looking out through the rear window. The driver of the car was also very surveillance-aware; he drove in excess of 100 miles per hour in the outside lane for some miles, only to suddenly pull over into the near-side lane in front of an articulated lorry and slam on his brakes, reducing his speed to 30 mph. The FSU vehicles immediately following him had no alternative but to overtake and by the time we got to the motorway services just north of Bristol we only had two vehicles that had not been compromised and therefore we had to call off the operation.

This did however persuade the FSU that the gang we were dealing with justified the attention of their more experienced 'A' team. I spent several days with them, and on 9 July, Woody was picked up and followed from Ladywood by the surveillance team. With others he went to an address in Kingstanding, where they picked up another member of the team. We belted down the A449. They went directly from there to Kidderminster, where they got in to a storage unit of an electrical shop and stole two video recorders. They had obviously checked this place out before because they knew exactly where they were going and how to get in. They didn't need to break in because security was very lax; as far as I remember they simply walked in and took the items.

They travelled back to Kingstanding to another address on College Road, where they delivered the two stolen video recorders. They then drove off up College Road towards Hawthorn Road, sharp left into Weycroft Road and we forced them to stop at the junction with Broomhill Road. My grandparents used to live in Kingstanding so I know the area reasonably well. Unfortunately my arrest of Woody and the other people in the car was witnessed by somebody who knew him, who walked back to the handler's house and told him what he had seen. I'm not sure whether this was intentional or just coincidental but the handler was alerted. Fortunately the FSU had left somebody watching his house and they saw him go back inside for the video recorders, hand one of them over to this passer-by and take the other one to a photography shop opposite. We found out later that the handler's mother worked there. By this time I was on my way to Erdington Police Station with the ones I had arrested so I had to get back to the scene to arrest the passer-by.

The operation yielded five other arrests on suspicion of receiving stolen property: targets 'Abbey', 'Ken', 'Pepper', 'Poet', and 'Gerry', but there was no suggestion that these individuals were linked to the Zulus' public order activities.

*

We had eight formal meetings with the Crown Prosecution Service as the operation progressed, including a key meeting involving an assistant chief constable on 23 June and a critical meeting on 24 September, much closer to 'D-Day', to discuss proposals for search warrants, initial objections to legal representation, possible objections to bail, and the court process to be followed after the first major phase of arrests. This early contact proved crucial when we came under scrutiny following the collapse of other hooligan trials in London, and the CPS publicly said there would be no special review of our work: 'We have no reason to think that similar problems exist in Red Card,' they said. We had evidence against people for a number of crimes. In the main it was evidence that officers had witnessed personally or had filmed. We also had verbal evidence about previous incidents, and evidence of arrangements made for disorder planned in the future.

October 7 was set provisionally as the day on which we would launch a wave of co-ordinated arrests. Though the weight of evidence had been gathering impressive momentum, we still had to question if there was enough of it on which to secure convictions, based on reasonable probability and doubt, against the public interest need of stopping the gang from running amok and the possibility that more innocent people would be terrorised.

A detailed Operational Order was prepared, no mean feat as our needs determined that a total of 183 officers were to be involved in the first arrests. This phase would be carried out at addresses in Staffordshire, the West Mercia force area and the West Midlands. Most of the officers were from the West Midlands Police with a small contingent from the British Transport Police, the force that I had joined as a cadet in 1968. I still had a great deal of affection and respect for them.

There was minute attention to detail, with 'dress of the day' for uniform staff being 'NATO style' jumpers, and car coats to be worn for inclement weather. All officers were instructed to carry a torch. I smile as I think of this because today's policing style is far different and even getting police officers to wear a flat cap or a helmet seems to be a challenge these days. We also handed out meal tickets for the officers to be fed later on. They say that armies march on their stomachs and this is equally true of police officers, who would face bricks and bottles without a gripe but would complain bitterly if they were not fed. It's ironic to think that success or failure could sometimes rest on a full English breakfast to raise energy as well as motivation levels.

The other key issue was that of giving direction. In my experience police officers will always find something to complain about, but they will be most vocal if they don't get clear orders and direction. They might not like what they get told to do but they hate uncertainty and wishy-washy behaviour from senior officers who use management-speak to mask uncertainty. They needed to be pointed in the right direction before the arrow was fired.

The CID officers and sergeants from the Force Operational Support Unit, who were to be involved in the arrest and interview of targets, would be briefed the day before, a Tuesday, at 11.30 a.m. in the lecture theatre of Tally Ho Police Training Centre. Police officers are by nature sceptical and will always have a list of 'what if?' questions ready for such occasions; therefore it was imperative to the success of Operation Red Card to get these officers onside, motivated and fully prepared. The briefing lasted for some five hours and officers were allowed to retain their paperwork, with the exception of search warrants. These had been taken out before Birmingham Magistrates the previous Friday for each target address we intended to visit. Incident room staff worked tremendously hard typing up all of the necessary paperwork for a total of forty warrants, checking and double-checking them for mistakes. We couldn't afford any errors, and that certainly included calling on wrong addresses – which would cause serious embarrassment and probably formal complaints too.

> **ALEX:** Mike wanted to make sure that all of the targets lived where we thought they lived so that there were no problems with the warrants. When we weren't out on the streets he had us sitting up on addresses in small box vans until we got a confirmed sighting. It was boring work and one day we were parked up at the home address of one of the B Team. I got pissed off waiting around so got out of the van and tapped on his window loudly. The target came to the window to look outside. Job done and we left.

Had I known of this particular tactic at the time, I would have bollocked Alex accordingly but quietly applauded his initiative!

Naturally I was very pleased when the process was complete and the magistrates had approved all of the applied-for warrants without any problems. Having said that, DS Steve Trenbirth was the officer assigned to this specific task and its completion was less straightforward than either of us had first anticipated:

> **STEVE TRENBIRTH:** I went to get all the search warrants from the Magistrates Court. I thought I would be in and out quite quickly and that it would be a bit of a rubber stamp job once I had outlined the circumstances. As it was, the Magistrate and the Magistrates Clerk made me go through each address in detail to prove that we knew who lived there and what the individual grounds for the warrant application were. In fair-

ness they could see that this was a big job and clearly wanted to make sure that everything was right. I was there for about two hours.

That night I attended a chief inspector's retirement function and enjoyed a few well-earned pints. The excitement was mounting as our first arrest phase loomed. Whilst the advance briefing could have posed the risk of a leak about the planned arrest phase, thankfully there were no issues to contend with at all, just a positivity and buzz of anticipation among the staff. Early on the morning of 6 October, the day before the big arrest phase, the Incident Room at Bridge Street West Police Station was busy with us making late preparations for the CID briefing. There were covert officers sorting out the evidence packages and checking them, Mark the spotter sat watching intently some video footage while I, in a suit, with full beard and (nearly) full head of hair, got ready for my speaking part at the briefing. A door to one of the small offices was covered in jokes and sayings as quoted by Reece. It was his door.

The full team was present later that morning in the lecture theatre at the Tally Ho Police Training Centre, and was headed by some of the police top brass: Chief Inspector Ian Garrett, Detective Superintendent Roy Taylor and Chief Superintendent Clive Roche. I addressed my seated audience and started off by reading out the Operation Red Card number of each target and then verbally checking that the chosen CID officer for each of them was present. In a way it was a straightforward roll call, except that these were extraordinary circumstances and, for many of us, this was a momentous time. The room was packed and all listened intently. Target 1 'belonged' to Barrie, for instance, who replied, 'Here,' when I read out his name. Forty times I read out targets and officers, and forty affirmative replies came back. While I was working, Chief Superintendent Roche was pacing up and down, in uniform, impatient to get started. At that point the CID officers had little or no idea why they were there. But I had a process and he knew he had to wait for me to complete it. Finally, his time arrived and he opened the briefing.

He outlined the hooligan problem infesting Birmingham, and the recent history of the Zulu Warriors in 1986 and 1987. He mentioned their organised shoplifting and their notoriety among city centre licensees. He told them about the previous New Year, when more than sixty police officers had been confronted by a crowd chanting 'Zulu' and that within ten minutes two people had been stabbed. His view was that CCTV cameras at Birmingham City's St Andrew's football ground had caused the displacement of this group to the city centre. He mentioned a match against Huddersfield Town where all of the gang were in the pub and didn't even bother to go to the ground.

This operation, he stressed, was a joint one with the British Transport Police and the biggest of its type so far. Finally he mentioned the undercover officers and then asked each of them to stand up so the rest of the theatre attendees could see them, commenting that they had 'worked on the fringes of this group without warrant cards' and had 'lived on their wits', joking that today they looked cleaner than normal, which raised some laughter. This was a great piece of theatre on his part but also a nice touch and a moment when the under-cover officers could feel truly recognised for their efforts. He concluded by saying, 'You could all well do without getting up for 4 a.m. tomorrow but I hope that you will have been pleased to have been part of the inquiry. Thank you.' Then, almost as an afterthought, he said, 'Sergeant Layton assures me that we have better video evidence than on the other operations. Is that right?' I replied, 'I will let you know after tomorrow,' which brought more laughter from the room.

Then it was my turn to go into more detail. The adrenalin flowed strongly but I managed to keep my composure. I went on to talk at length about our group of targets within the whole Zulu Warriors gang. I used no notes throughout, only a wall chart with the targets on as a prompt if I needed it. I didn't need notes, I had lived with Operation Red Card for months and I knew the story inside out. The room remained quiet. People were focused. My left hand complemented my talking while my right stayed in my pocket for the duration. My final comments were that some arrest teams consisted of three officers, some of four, some of five and in one case six as 'the target has hands like shovels!' More laughter, which I was pleased to hear. I mentioned that in the main we felt that the evidence was strong against thirty-five of the forty targets, but less so against the other five.

Detective Superintendent Taylor briefed the CID officers on legal aspects of the case and mentioned that Francis had been involved in at least seven incidents as a planner or active participant and that we had a core group of thirteen that we were looking at for conspiracy. We were going to make use of a new Public Order Act that had come into force on 1 April that referred to affray and violent disorder. Much mirth was inadvertently caused too when Roy referred to a number of the Zulus being involved in offences of shoplifting and in particular 'screaming' in shops in the city centre. He quickly corrected himself to offences of 'steaming'. It was a moment of weird fun where I suddenly had a vision of lots of tough hooligans running around department stores and screaming, like a scene from St Trinians. Back in serious vein, he then explained that the press were going to be briefed beforehand about the arrest phase. Some people in the room shook their heads, to which he responded forcefully, 'It is semi-political and about public relations. It's gone to the highest level and that's how it is going to be.' He then explained that search warrants would be available under the Police and Criminal Evidence Act, emphasising that only minimum force should be used and the need to avoid smashing doors down and the like, with the comment, 'Remember they are the cowboys and Indians, not us.'

As the meeting approached its close, Chief Superintendent Roche made mention of the fact that the operation had originally been called Rorke's Drift but it had been changed, and rightly so, because of the Handsworth Riots (of 1981 and 1985). In the aftermath of those riots, mention had been made that standing at the barricades was like Rorke's Drift for the officers involved, an inappropriate comment which had attracted criticism from the local community, something which our football hooliganism operation certainly did not need, hence the name change. This was not an issue of race in any way. He then quipped, at my expense, 'Sergeant Layton is confused as he doesn't know where he is now!' More laughter but a sign of the relaxed relationship I had with him.

Just before 5 p.m. that day came the press briefing. At least eleven journalists from television and radio stations were present, notebooks at the ready, in a room at Force Headquarters. With tea and biscuits served, it was all very civilised. The Force press officer, Superintendent Martin Burton, was there along with Clive Roche, who briefed them all on the imminent job. They were joined by Roy Taylor and ACC Leopold, which was probably too many cooks as they slightly over-emphasised the fact that the news was embargoed until they gave the press permission to release it. Anyway, it was eventually decided that the news could be officially released no earlier than 9 a.m. and that they could film the briefing next morning at Tally Ho. A request to interview the undercover officers was declined on the basis that it was too risky for the safety of those officers. It was also agreed that a press conference would be held at 10 a.m. where any weapons or other items of interest recovered during the arrest phase would be displayed. Members of the media pushed for access to go out with arrest teams too but police concerns were raised about the use of high-density lighting for cameras in areas where we might get a negative reaction from the community. That decision was deferred until the morning of the arrests.

And so, on that day, the press conference called for by senior command team officers went ahead. The media were given an outline of the operation, and an embargo was placed on any reporting until an agreed time the following day, to be determined by the position with regard to the arrest of offenders. The press conference was another calculated risk but an essential one if we wanted to achieve maximum coverage for Red Card. It was very important for the citizens of Birmingham to be aware that we were doing our utmost for them against a strong and highly dangerous and irresponsible set of, yes, villains.

The full-scale briefing for staff, at 4.45 a.m. on 7 October, was to take place in the ballroom of the Tally Ho Police Training Centre in Edgbaston. A seating plan was drawn up before the arrival of officers, who would be placed in a number of different arrest teams. Even experienced officers don't always function that well during the early hours of the morning and we wanted to organise them into their respective teams with the minimum of fuss. Each chair was marked with the officer's name and they were placed next to their 'new' team members. Many of them had never met each other before and they would be coming from all parts of the West Midlands.

CHAPTER 11

DAWN RAIDS

THE DOZENS OF bleary-eyed but keyed-up police officers filtering into the ballroom of the Tally Ho Training Centre at the ungodly hour of 4.30 a.m. were greeted by row upon row of pink-backed chairs facing a stage. I was at the front with Chief Inspector Ian Garrett, doing a last-minute check of all the paperwork. Cameras were clicking at the side of the stage and TV cameras and lights shone brightly from the back of the room.

The main briefing was given by my divisional chief superintendent, Clive Roche, and lasted fifteen minutes. The room was a mix of uniformed and plain-clothes officers all listening intently, if in a few cases still a little dozily. 'There is less opportunity for football hooligans to commit violence in the ground,' he began. 'We have noticed a displacement of that violence into the city centre. That is why we've conducted this covert operation for the last eight months. Today we will be executing some thirty-five warrants on the houses of the main people involved in the offences. These range from serious public order offences to affray, wounding, theft and all sorts of other offences.' Afterwards, evidence packages were handed out to the arrest teams. This entailed my shouting out the target numbers, one by one, and it became quite monotonous as we had forty numbers to shout out and forty packages to distribute, but again it had to be watertight.

Our contingency planning had worked well and all the assigned officers were despatched out into the dark and a cold morning rain. Happily for the reporters there, the decision had been made that they could in fact go out with arrest teams, as long as they did not go into any suspects' premises, did not use high-density lights outside and did exactly as they were told by the police. They were not, under any circumstances, to show the faces of any of the targets. ITN (Independent Television News, then the BBC's main rival) went out to Milk Race's address in Bordesley Green while another news team went to an address in Pretoria Road where Checkers and Red lived. The Daily News went to Hoops' address in Druids Heath, and the Birmingham Post and Evening Mail to Light's address in Warley. Central TV went to the Zulus' unofficial photographer Shirt Out's address in Rubery and the BBC and Express and Star to Elm's address in Sheldon. The remainder of the attendant media set up outside Steelhouse Lane Police Station, ready to film, take photos and compile notes on the events as they took place.

A line of pruned rose bushes at the front of the house of Shirt Out, together with an empty hanging basket, seemed to emphasise the bleakness of the suspect's situation. Officers led him away with a blanket over his head to Digbeth Police Station. One of them was assigned officer Bryan Dorrian.

BRYAN DORRIAN: At that time, I was attached to a local burglary team at Bournville Police Station. Everyone just knew me as 'BD'. I hadn't been involved in any legwork leading up to the first arrest phase of Red Card. I was just nominated for one of the arrest teams. I went out with three other officers. One of them was a guy called Roger who sadly is no longer with us. He was a dog handler but also attached to the burglary team. The other two officers were in uniform. We had a reporter in the police transit van with us and I did an interview en route to our target's address in Rubery. We had no problems at all when we got to the house and it was Roger who said, 'Bingo, Bryan!' when we found the photograph albums containing scenes of football violence.

As one media outlet subsequently described it, our first intention was to 'arrive before the milk' at target addresses, quietly and swiftly and without drama. Richard Lutz, a reporter for Central News, described the scene of the briefing that morning: 'It's a pre-dawn briefing for a hundred and eighty policemen. Their mission, Operation Red Card. Their goal, to smash the Zulu Warriors, a vicious gang linked with Birmingham City Football Club. Their violence has now spread to the city centre and police want to round up the ringleaders.'

The nominated exhibits officer for the arrest phase was Detective Sergeant Ken Dear. His responsibilities included the receipt, documentation and storage of all of the evidence exhibits brought in by the arrest teams. Property was listed in books with a yellow copy and was retained in wardrobes with target names attached in a secure room. Each team also had its own exhibits officer who logged and referenced each item of clothing, weaponry, newspaper cuttings and so on. Whoever took possession of the item would create a label bearing the initials of the officer who found it, sequentially numbered, such as ML/1, ML/2, etc. Items were to be bagged up in clear plastic bags or brown paper packaging and then handed to Ken Dear with the labels attached. There were to be hundreds of exhibits so it was crucial that the procedure was followed precisely.

The BTP liaison officer on the day of the arrests was Inspector Hackett. He had a fairly minor role in the control room but we needed him there to deal with any BTP-related crimes on the railway or requests for additional resources. The logistics officer was Acting Inspector John White. He had a challenging job to do but his great enthusiasm was a big help. His duties included ensuring that all of the teams deployed were aware of exactly where and when to turn up and which vehicles they were assigned to. He also had to arrange all the meal times as well as collate every officer's overtime incurred, and to address any welfare issues arising on the day. He was a jovial character but extremely well organised and good at keeping people focused on their roles. In the control room, last but by no means least, the constable assigned the task of plotting the names of people as they were arrested was Mick Rollins.

Outside the Tally Ho Centre, we had officers on car parking duties, with forty police vehicles duly positioned and the keys in the ignition ready for the anticipated sharp exits. A call sign was placed in each windscreen for the team that vehicle had been assigned to. We left nothing to chance; everything had to be supremely well organised and tight. It would be costly not only in financial terms but in physical terms too if anything went wrong due to poor preparation. The sight of nineteen police transit vans lined up in rows was impressive. The journalists stuck to their deal that they could go out with certain arrest teams so long as they did not get in the way, enter premises or reveal any identities of those arrested, and blankets and coats were on hand to conceal the heads of some suspects as they were escorted away anyway. As a result of this favourable partnership with the media, Red Card would receive significant local and national press, radio and television coverage.

I put myself in the Force Control Room at Lloyd House, the West Midlands Police headquarters, also known for the duration as Alpha Control. It was physically set up the day before, on the afternoon of 6 October. All of the targets' profiles were put up on huge dry-wipe boards in front of the rows of empty desks, ready for the next day. And today was that day. It had been open from 4.45 a.m. and everything was in place when I arrived. Seated directly behind me were my detective superintendent, Roy Taylor, my divisional chief superintendent, and Assistant Chief Constable (Operations) Paul Leopold, all no-nonsense, hard taskmasters – so no pressure on me then! With the names of all forty targets on the dry-wipe boards, we had an officer whose sole job was to act as a 'plotter', updating the boards as the day progressed and as news came in. It looked a little like Bomber Command in World War II, as portrayed in films like The Battle Of Britain.

I waited anxiously for the update calls to start coming in from the arrest teams, using two dedicated radio channels and hand-held units known as PFX radios, to our radio operators. The force operated on a number of channels for normal daily business and they were routinely busy, leaving insufficient air time free for an arrest operation of this scale; the officers on the ground simply would not have been able to get their messages through to the controller. Normally the procedure was rather convoluted: officers had to book on the air when you went out on a mission, then confirm 'plus TA' (your time of arrival) when you got there, then provide an update if an arrest was made, then let the controller know when you were leaving, and then confirm another TA when you got back to the station. For the arrest phase, using PFX radios gave us the capacity to use spare channels dedicated to specific stand-alone operations such as ours. The trick today was handing one out to each team at the beginning of the day and getting them all back safe and sound at the end. All of the teams' call signs were prefixed Romeo Delta (signifying the letters RD) plus the individual target number they were to arrest. Our main target, Francis, from the Washwood Heath area, had the distinction of being Romeo Delta One.

This was the day I had been waiting for and anticipating for many months. I almost prayed it would all go according to plan but I had no way of actually knowing until whatever news was radioed back to us. All I could do was to sit and wait. I wasn't up for talking too much at this point. I no longer had any control over events and didn't much like the feeling. Fortunately we did not have to wait long: soon after 'kick-off' time, calls began to arrive in the Control Room, and all of them with a positive result.

ANDY MURCOTT: We had forty targets and about the same number of addresses to visit. It was a 4.15 a.m. parade time for duty and I was allocated Green Hood, our number 2 on the target list and number 2 in the hierarchy of those we were looking at. Three of us went to his address in a CID car; our call sign was Romeo Delta Two. We hit the address early in the morning, still dark. He lived in Hodge Hill in East Birmingham, not an area I know well. I think it was a semi-detached house, built in the nineteen-thirties or thereabouts, and typical of the area. He was from a typical working-class family but not a criminal one. He was at home, with both his parents, and we didn't meet any resistance. I think we recovered some evidence of football violence, photograph albums, clothing and other paraphernalia. He behaved as though he was expecting a visit.

We took him to Queens Road Police Station. During the time I spent with him he mentioned that he had got into football violence because he was trying to emulate the success of his brother, who had won Cadet of the Year during his training as a Royal Marine. He didn't think he could ever achieve similar success but wanted an identity as an aggressor, but he recognised it was a poor substitute, or words to that effect.

Liam and DC Ian Mabbett both went to the home of target Oburn, who we also knew as the Diary Man or the Historian. He wasn't hard to identify. As Liam later said, 'At every single game he wore the same black V-neck jumper. He was even wearing it when he was arrested. It must have been the only one he had.'

IAN MABBETT: My target lived in Shirley and after the briefing I made my way there with two other uniform officers. We were not expecting trouble. It was a beautiful home and a lovely family. His parents were devastated and told him to make sure that he was honest with us. He was quiet and polite. I think that he was in shock. We searched his bedroom and almost immediately found two diaries in his dressing table drawer with some football programmes. A quick look showed that they contained lots of detail about football violence. We took him to Bournville Police Station and booked him in. When I interviewed him I was always concerned about getting to the facts. He could write what he liked in his diaries and I was concerned about what was reality and what was bravado. He tried to put himself on the fringe of things but did say something about once going with an advance party so that that they could see what the police tactics were. He used a phrase 'saturation policing' which I thought was strange at the time, as it was a police phrase. He had a good job working with computers and I actually met his boss once who said that he couldn't believe it when he realised that he had been involved.

Two published accounts of the first arrest phase, from the newspaper reporters invited along, capture the flavour of that day:

I accompanied a detective and three constables on a swoop to detain one of the men suspected of major offences. Our target was a smart semi-detached in Sheldon and we drove there in unmarked cars. The police team parked round the corner from the house and one of the uniform officers climbed into the back garden in case the suspect tried to make a getaway. The detective knocked on the front door and seconds later a woman opened a bedroom window and agreed to let the officers in. The team, who had a search warrant, were admitted to the house at 5.20 a.m. and after waking up the suspect, who was still in bed, they searched for weapons. Half an hour later they emerged with the man – believed to be in his early twenties. He had a coat over his head to protect his identity and walked quietly to their car. The officers then drove him to Bromford Lane Police Station for questioning.

At one address in a sprawling estate in Druids Heath, the police van was parked about 100 yards from the target house. Four officers – two in uniform – prepared to swoop on the terraced home and arrest the suspect. One officer covered the back entrance, while the others knocked loudly on the front door. It was opened by a middle aged man who was shown a warrant – without any commotion he allowed police to enter the house. About forty minutes later the police emerged with their suspect, his head covered in a blanket. The man was bundled into the van and taken at high speed to Digbeth Police Station for questioning.

There is nothing glamorous about making an arrest. Taking away someone's liberty is a serious issue and if you, as the police, don't get the process right then legal challenges will follow. The arrest of Francis was no different: rarely are such procedures as straightforward or as simple as we would prefer. At about 5.25 a.m., six loud knocks were made on the half-glazed door of the house in Warren Road, Washwood Heath. Some officers were already at the back of the property to head off any attempted escape. The door was quickly opened by Francis, who was wearing a white top. DS Barrie Davies had been assigned to this particular mission.

BARRIE DAVIES: I worked with Mike when he was a detective sergeant in the summer of 1983 and I was attached to the CID. A lot of the Red Card targets were about at that time and we were catching them for shoplifting in Birmingham city centre and elsewhere. I knew Fats and Cab well. They were heavily into designer gear and whilst the police were tied up after a game they would do some 'steaming' – shoplifting in large groups. I also recall another West Indian youth who was a Zulu called Skinny. After I finished my CID attachment I was back in uniform for a while and Fats used to take the piss out of me because of this when he saw me out and about in the city.

It was in 1983–84, I was in uniform in New Street showing a new PC around. It was one of his first days out. Plymouth Argyle were playing, I think Watford, at Villa Park in a cup semi-final. There were two or three Plymouth fans wearing green and white scarves in Stephenson Place and suddenly a huge Zulu shout went up from nearby. It was just like Rorke's Drift in the film. I looked up and there was about two hundred Zulus standing at the top of the ramp which leads into the

Birmingham Shopping Centre. They had come out of a pub there. I thought, Jesus, we are in the shit, and I called for back-up. I ran to the Plymouth fans and told them to clear off quick. Fortunately our vans turned up in seconds and the Zulus just melted away.

On the arrest day, Barrie introduced himself at the address of Francis and then entered the house with the three other, uniformed officers in attendance. It was quickly established that there was no one else at home. Barrie told our target, 'From this moment on you are under arrest on suspicion of conspiracy with others between 1986 and 1987 to commit violent disorder in the Birmingham, West Midlands Police area. You do not have to say anything unless you wish to do so but what you say may be given in evidence. Do you understand?' He replied, 'Yes,' in a subdued but calm tone.

Barrie asked, 'Can you get yourself dressed and you will be taken to Steelhouse Lane Police Station?'

Francis looked thoughtful for a moment before replying 'Yes' again.

He was then told, 'I also have a search warrant to search for clothing and any other items of evidence which may support the charges against you. I have a copy here for you.'

Francis then confirmed no one else was living at the address. He got dressed and combed his hair and was given time to find a telephone number for his solicitor before being handcuffed to a uniformed officer and led from the room. He explained to the officers how to lock the outside doors of the premises, commenting on how expensive they were. He maintained a quiet dignity throughout, appearing resigned to his fate and not scared of it. A search started of the rooms in the house, which were dark and generally unwelcoming with few vestiges of personal or a family life but were clean and relatively neat, even if the wallpaper was flowery and dated. The search was methodical and we created a detailed record for every item we seized. Drawers were removed from the wardrobe and the contents examined. The drawers were even turned upside down to make sure that nothing was taped to them. Clothing was examined and there was no evidence of a glamorous lifestyle, though some of his boots had reinforced toecaps. And despite the numerous made-up television and film drama scenes contradicting it, our officers ensured that everything was meticulously put back exactly as it was found.

A radio call then came in from Alpha Control requesting an update. The reply: 'One in custody. Searching premises now.' The officers checked to see if there was a loft. Some group photographs were examined: lads out on the town and a newspaper cutting about an incident at the Manor pub in Station Road, Stechford, in January 1987. Address books were examined as well as a gold ring, and as the wardrobe was moved a stash of adult books was found. That did not represent an offence though and so the house was secured and left in its own silence. Francis was taken to Steelhouse Lane Police Station. Before he left the police vehicle, his head was covered with a police jacket to prevent the waiting press photographers from taking a picture of his face. As he was led up the stairs into the station by two officers, one of them counted out each step to avoid the suspect tripping up. He was guided into the passageway leading to the custody area. Seated on one of the benches was another suspect with his head down between his hands. Four uniformed officers stood around him. Francis avoided eye contact as he was led past.

By the end of that day, thirty-nine of our targets were in custody at designated stations around the West Midlands, namely Steelhouse Lane, Digbeth, Stechford, Bromford Lane, Bournville Lane and Queens Road. We had put a lot of thought into how targets would be grouped at different stations and the skills of the officers who were nominated to interview them. I also placed one of the undercover officers at each of the police stations to act as liaison. They were instructed to stay firmly in the background and under no circumstances to come into contact with any of the arrested individuals, but I also sensed how important it was for them to feel part of events that day. Plus it served as a signal for the start of 'closure' for them in their undercover guises.

The two overt officers from Red Card helped to view the visual evidence at the two stations where we were to house some of our most prominent targets. They knew and understood the material intimately and I trusted them completely to make the most of it. I also knew that they would take some pleasure from watching the faces of individuals as they were shown being caught on camera. They didn't let me down.

All the officers had been briefed that due regard must be given at all times to the requirements of the Police And Criminal Evidence Act 1984. In consulatation with the Crown Prosecution Service, we decided to deny access to legal advice during the very early stages. This was nothing untoward or drastic, no civil rights or liberties were infringed upon; we only had the success of the operation in mind. We hoped to minimise the risk of others not yet arrested being alerted indirectly by those who had, or evidence connected to serious arrestable offences suddenly being 'lost'. As the day wore on, those in custody were allowed to see solicitors where requested. Our potentially contentious policy was never challenged at the subsequent court hearings and our intentions were entirely moral and legal.

In addition, three others were arrested, one on suspicion of burglary, one previously unidentified target, and a target who we had planned to arrest later. By the close of this first phase, it was time for quiet satisfaction and huge relief, I felt that all of my personal efforts had been vindicated, and to effect the arrest of such a large number of people, with only one exception, showed that all of the meticulous planning had been worth it. All of my tiredness was disappearing rapidly and the thought of a pint in the bar seemed very attractive. And that one remaining target would be arrested the following day.

CHAPTER 12

BLOWING THE WHISTLE

OFFICERS GATHERED FOR the post-arrest debrief session in the lecture theatre at Tally Ho Centre at 12.45 p.m. The white transit vans of the West Midlands Police were parked up outside along with a royal-blue British Transport Police van bearing the force crest. It was raining, cool and overcast but inside the centre the mood was now much lighter.

I again stood at the front of the room, together with Roy Taylor. I had prepared the huge dry-wipe board so that I could make notes on it as we went along. For the briefing the day before I had kept my suit jacket on but now it was jacket off and shirt sleeves rolled up. It was time to see what we had discovered and learned from the searches and initial interviews. I was still up for it, feeling fresh and motivated. We had all been up since the early hours but there was no sense of tiredness for me or the others in the crowded theatre. Police officers deal with fatigue in different ways and often lean towards humour to lighten the mood and to relax. This particular occasion was, however, deadly serious. We already had a lot of visual and covert evidence; now was the time to see whether we had managed to get the so-called icing on the cake. We commenced the debriefing, going through the process one at a time by calling out the name of each Red Card target and asking for an update from the officers dealing with each one.

First up was Francis. He had faced a general interview to confirm his background details followed by a discussion about the structure of the Zulu Warriors. He had claimed to be actually the current second in command and not the leader in the organisation, which had its own structure, each member having a place in the ladder with certain people having specific roles. Their rules were that they did not attack ordinary people in the street randomly, did not attack women and children, and only attacked opposition fans by arrangement with them. At his address we found prison letters from an individual who clearly regarded himself as the Zulus' main man, signing the letter 'The Guvenor'; he was allegedly involved in the attack on PC Harry Doyle too. We also found that Francis possessed a diary with names and telephone numbers for some of the other Zulu targets. He had already admitted being involved in the Hill Street incident, where the Tottenham youth was stabbed and seriously wounded, and we found him quite talkative, probably because he was intelligent enough to realise there was no point in making any denials – we had him 'bang to rights' as the saying went. He tried making the point that lots of kids were going around and innocently chanting 'Zulu', but that was not the case in our experience. Somewhat ironically, a photograph was recovered which showed him with quite severe facial injuries from an attack that appeared to be the subject of a criminal injuries compensation claim back in March 1986.

Up next was target number 2, Green Hood, who had admitted being present at the Hill Street incident and said that he had been a member of the Zulus for about four years. He did not think that he deserved to be seen as one of the ringleaders as there were people 'far better' than him. He had admitted to being present at the fight at The Cabin when Aston Villa fans were attacked, and to a part in its orchestration, but claimed to have left when the attack actually began. He also had at his address a newspaper cutting which showed him on the pitch on the day of the Leeds Riot in 1985, as well as photographs of other targets.

Our number 3 target, Milk Race, followed. During the debrief it became clear that he had been involved in a very frank and open discussion about his involvement with the Zulus. This was a fine start in our ambitions to make the Zulus pay, with three of our high profile figures providing crucial evidence and testimonies. And there was more to come. Unfortunately, some of it came much later than we had hoped it would, such as evidence two years further on, showing that Francis, Red, Sidekick, Green Hood, Shirt Out and Ant were involved in disturbances on the day of the 1985 riot, in the city centre or at the football ground.

Target 5, Raincoat, admitted being in the fight at Hill Street and to throwing a glass. He also admitted going in the Mini car to the Craven Arms to arrange the fight with Tottenham's hooligans beforehand. Number 28, Grease Head, admitted his involvement in Hill Street but denied being a Zulu, claiming he had only been to two away games. He did own up to having some knowledge about the disorder at the Edgbaston

Cricket Ground. More resistance during questioning came from target 25, Hoop. In the words of the interviewing officer and much to the amusement of the audience, Hoop admitted to the day of the week and to his name but otherwise denied absolutely everything.

Target number 24, Light, denied being a Zulu but admitted that he was quite prepared to have 'a knock' if there were ever some opposition fans around at the match. He admitted fighting at Hill Street and to standing outside The Fox whilst others put the pub's windows through. He also put himself at the fight in Manzoni Gardens involving Stoke followers and the disorder at the Aston Villa game.

Shirt Out, twenty-first on our list, was next. As he was known as the gang's photographer too, Roy Taylor quipped that we should get him in to take a photo of proceedings. Shirt Out admitted being part of the Leeds Riot in 1985 and taking the photos of the Australian Bar being smashed up prior to the horrendous events at St Andrew's that day. He also admitted involvement in the incidents at Hill Street and The Fox, and to being part of the fight in the park at Plymouth Argyle. He confirmed that he was in town on the day of The Cabin violence but claimed that the bouncers would not let him into the premises when he tried to enter. As the Zulus' unofficial photographer, he possessed many photographs and press cuttings relating to their actions and also letters from 'The Guvenor'.

Number 8, Sidekick, admitted being at the Leeds riot as well as involvement in the Hill Street and The Fox incidents. Midwest also admitted Hill Street, as did Turn Up, who confessed to being a Zulu but only as just 'a soldier'. Target number 61, 'Frown', denied being a Zulu but admitted to knowing Midwest and Turn Up and to involvement in the Hill Street and some other instances of disorder.

Target 12, Orange, admitted knowing various Zulus and to being a part of the Hill Street trouble. He denied The Cabin incident but knew who had organised it. Recovered from his bedroom was a piece of 12-inch piping while the police had already found items of identifiable/incriminating clothing. Orange had been attacked in the Monte Carlo nightclub in the Handsworth area of Birmingham and had been slashed on the arm. Someone had been arrested for the crime and a bloodstained top was kept as an exhibit at Thornhill Road Police Station.

Checkers (target 13) was another one who smiled a lot while admitting only what day of the week it was. Number 31, Wax, admitted involvement in The Fox and Hill Street disturbances, while 32, Style, did admit to possessing a cosh while at Hill Street – and hitting someone with it – but said that it was one which he had 'picked up off the floor'. He claimed not to be an out-and-out Zulu, although five Zulu Warrior calling cards were found at his home. For some unknown reason, he also had a photograph of target 41, Harry, 'mooning' the camera – not a pretty sight!

Target number 50, Sharp, claimed an unusual defence which caused considerable mirth amongst the officers: 'I am not a Zulu Warrior, just a football hooligan.' He admitted his part in the disorder at the Hull City game, when a mob had attempted to lure one of our inspectors into a trap so as to assault him. He also confessed to throwing stones at the Stoke City supporters' coaches outside the Watering Hole pub near St Andrew's. Target 53, Benetton, also admitted involvement in the Hull City incident as well as being present when the missiles were thrown at the Stoke coaches. He also admitted hanging around after the games specifically looking for trouble.

Number 55, Grace, owned up to a prominent role in the Hull City incidents; he had intended dragging a police officer into the mob to give him a beating and therefore making a nice entry for his own diary about having a punch-up on the Spion Kop of St Andrew's. Target 51, Goofy, owned up to the Hull incident too, as well as throwing stones at the Stoke coaches and to the fight at Werneth train station, where he saw someone wielding an iron bar. Target 48, Sleepy, confessed to being part of the fight, with fifty others, at Werneth too. Target number 49, nicknamed Dal, also admitted his part in the fight at Werneth as well as seeing Bruno kicking someone while they were on the floor.

Target number 56, Comedian, maintained that he was not a Zulu but rather a part of a group called the 'Party Timers', which in essence consisted of members of the B Team. He admitted opening train doors while the train was at speed and expressed some remorse for his dangerous actions. Target 58 was the man known as the group's historian or 'Diary Man', christened by us as Oburn. He was the subject of much discussion, primarily because of the detailed notebooks he had written, and I jokingly suggested that we should start using his skills to compile and improve our own intelligence reports.

Number 62, Mop, maintained that he was not a Zulu Warrior and that in fact every Birmingham Zulu was black. In his bedroom, however, which had no wallpaper and was not described in the most complimentary terms ('a dump'), he had 'Zulus' painted on the wall and a Union flag with BCFC written across it. He admitted wandering around with the B Team after games and that whilst they were looking for trouble, he was just there to look after them. He denied all the covert evidence put to him but when questioned about an incident where stones were thrown at four mounted police officers, he interrupted to say, 'No, there was five of them,' sparking more chuckles from the audience.

Target 43, Gingerbeard, admitted being present outside The Fox pub when the fight occurred and went on to describe two other fights, one in Torquay at a pub between rival fans and the one at Plymouth where seventy Blues ran at two hundred Argyle fans. He knew the whole structure of the Zulu gang and he drank with them. Meanwhile, 45, Specs, denied any involvement of a criminal nature but admitted that he was at Plymouth and liked to stay with the groups as they provided a sense of protection. He suggested that he liked seeing them fighting as it 'excited him'. Target 75, Sheet, was consistently denying any involvement in anything. We did consider him to be a more peripheral player but that certainly did not equate to no involvement. Our tenth target, Elm, was another matter; he was talking relatively freely to us and had alluded to committing a robbery in Torquay.

At the time of this whole debriefing session, we were still on the hunt for a couple of targets and a few were still being interviewed but we all believed, probably knew, it had been a very good start. At 2 p.m. the officers were despatched from the lecture theatre to carry on with further interviews and to finalise the charges against the suspects. The day was far from done, there was much work still, but it would be enjoyable and worthwhile and most certainly gratifying for us all.

Not everything had gone to plan with the arrest phase. One target who was not known in the public domain and has not featured in the story until now, was given the police nickname 'Sightseer' and was number 30. He was very much on the fringes, a twenty-three-year-old from Cannock in Staffordshire who was arrested in the first phase on suspicion of involvement in public order offences. He was taken to Digbeth Police Station, where the detective chief inspector, the nominated liaison officer for the day there, decided that there was insufficient evidence against him and so rejected the charge and released him. I did not agree with the decision but by the time I found out it was too late. I was far from impressed but I knew that I would not win an argument with a chief inspector and there was no point in putting his nose out of joint, as the time would come when I would return to normal CID work and senior officers had long memories.

Target number 37, nicknamed Wise, a twenty-three-year-old from Aston, was also taken to Digbeth Police Station on 7 October and was released initially on police bail but was not charged. A thirty-two-year-old from Bordesley Green was also taken to Digbeth Police Station and interviewed about an offence of criminal damage at Aston Villa's ground, for which no further action was taken. He was, however, charged in connection with an outstanding-fine commitment warrant and kept in custody. His target number was 40 and he was Meatloaf, the man who undercovers Colin and Adam had effectively befriended previously. Target 59, whose identity we already knew and hence who wasn't given a nickname, was ultimately fined for public order offences.

*

On 9 October, another of our targets, a twenty-year-old West Indian male from Bordesley Green who was already serving a custodial sentence, was interviewed, at HM Onley Detention Centre and charged with violent disorder over the 'Tottenham incident' at Hill Street. He was Cab, number 14 on our list, already convicted for an offence of wounding outside The Swan pub.

Cab had black curly hair, big eyebrows and a bit of a moustache. He was of medium build and a known shop-lifter, identifiable by his green padded anorak with mustard coloured lining in the hood. Outwardly a quiet individual, he was apparently not afraid of anyone. I knew him very well; he was part of an organised shoplifting team operating mainly in the city centre. For eight months in 1986, immediately before I took on the intelligence role, I managed the city centre Shoplifting Squad and got to know many of these lads. Their favourite tactic in stores and shops was to distract staff working there whilst one of the other thieves lifted a whole rail of clothes and dropped them into a black bin-liner bag held by a second person. They would be out of the shop in less than a minute and the merchandise transferred to holdalls at the ready nearby.

In May 1987, Cab had appeared at Birmingham Crown Court for sentencing for what Judge Kenneth Wilson Mellor described as the most ugly example of public violence that he had encountered, an attack that was akin to the sort of violence seen at football matches where people took delight in inflicting hurt on others. He was describing an attack on an eighteen-year-old outside The Swan pub in Coventry Road, Yardley, as he was leaving the premises at closing time. A group of men, including our target, attacked and wounded him. The eighteen-year-old was able to defend himself initially but after receiving repeated punches, kicks and blows with an iron bar, his resistance crumbled. He later needed sixteen stitches to head wounds and had cuts and bruises all over his body, while a man who went to his rescue had his jaw broken. Our target made off in a car with a second person, chased by police. The car was abandoned and Cab was arrested later in a park, hiding in bushes. When interviewed, he claimed that he had only been at the scene of the crime by chance and that because he knew some of the other youths he felt he should help them. He claimed to have only thrown a few punches at the victim.

Also connected to this case was a twenty-three-year-old Zulu Warrior who I knew equally well, notorious for his shoplifting skills. He wasn't particularly light on his feet but he was certainly light with his fingers. He was subsequently acquitted on the direction of the Judge on the basis of insufficient evidence, but Cab received nine months in youth custody, which is why he didn't feature again in our operation after the incident at Hill Street on 11 April, when he was also seen wielding a weapon. Because I knew him by name already, his fate was quickly sealed that day and he subsequently received a further term of twelve months' imprisonment, with nine months suspended for his involvement in the Hill Street disorder, having twice failed to attend court. He had complete disregard for the law and an intense dislike of the police which I could never fathom. What this clearly illustrated was that whilst we were successfully gathering evidence in Operation Red Card, certain targets were concurrently involved in other crimes in other parts of Birmingham and surrounds. In all this made for a total of forty-four people arrested in this initial phase of Red Card, their ages ranging from seventeen to forty years.

After his arrest on 7 October, it transpired that B Team target number 54, Dek, a twenty-two-year-old caster, was due to get married the following Saturday. After a plea for bail from his solicitor on his behalf, he was fortunate enough to be given the permission to complete his marriage vows. I dare say it was a wedding to remember, if not really for the right reasons. He was later fined for a public order offence at the Shrewsbury Town game in May.

CHAPTER 13

EXTRA TIME

A SECOND WAVE of Operation Red Card arrests was launched at 6 a.m. on 14 October. Thirty-five officers, who had been briefed the day before, brought in a further eight of our suspects and two previously unidentified targets. All of them were interviewed at Steelhouse Lane Police Station and charged with a variety of offences. Andy Murcott was again involved, going with a team of officers to arrest Woody again, this time for an offence of violent disorder: 'I can't remember the finer details other than that when I took his prisoner photograph in the cell block he had a big grin on his face.'

At the home of one twenty-year-old target, in Ward End, police officers recovered newspaper cuttings relating to the previous week's arrests stuck onto the bedroom walls, along with other cuttings going back as far as the Leeds match in 1985 saying 'Missiles, Mayhem and Sheer Madness', 'Blackest Day', and one headlined 'Shops hit by Zulu thieves'. Festooned across the whole of one wall was a large Union flag with 'Junior Business Boys BCFC' scrawled on it and on the bedroom door was another Union flag as well as business cards saying 'Junior Business Boys, Pride of the Midlands' and 'Zulu Warriors BCFC'. It was like a shrine to the ethos of violence, with the walls painted in bright red throughout. This individual, nicknamed 'Ant', would later receive a very long prison sentence in 1988 for wounding a Leeds United supporter with intent.

DS Barrie Davies, who would eventually retire at detective chief inspector level, arrested Fats that day.

BARRIE DAVIES: All he kept going on about was the Portsmouth 25 and how he was there and they stood in a line and held it toe-to-toe. He loved talking about it. He lived at home with his mother and she opened the door. We went upstairs and into his bedroom which smelt strongly of body odour. He was under the bedclothes and just looked out at me and said, 'No, not you again.' I said words to the effect of 'I'm not in uniform any more, I'm back on the CID and you're under arrest.' He wasn't smiling now. For a while he refused to get out of bed and I thought, how are we going to drag him down the stairs? He was so big. Finally he agreed to get dressed and as we left he shouted to his mother, 'Don't worry mum, I won't be long. They've got nothing on me.' At first there was some animosity between us and then he calmed down. I always found from negotiating with people that talking about football was a great leveller and it worked with him. Once he started talking we couldn't shut him up. He loved being part of it and kept on about being proud about being one of the Portsmouth twenty-five and that they had even had shirts made to show that they were there. He told us all about how they used to set up organised fights by sending a lieutenant out to meet up with the opposition to arrange things. He was quite open. They would sometimes decide to use weapons but mostly it was fists and boots.

The next day, another previously unidentified target was arrested, making a total of eleven arrests in this follow-up phase and giving us a final total of sixty-seven as a direct result of Red Card. In addition, covert officers found and obtained evidence in relation to unrelated offences of wounding and criminal damage, and five further arrests were made whilst overt officers were off duty, namely two for criminal damage and three for public order offences. I was extremely proud of the team and we had a quiet drink together that Friday to celebrate and to let the dust settle.

The following Monday, I was required to brief the Assistant Chief Constable (Operations) on the final outcome. He expressed his satisfaction with the operation, which was high praise in itself. During the course of the co-ordinated arrests, some three hundred and fifty exhibits had been seized. These included around a dozen knives – including craft knives, penknives and an ornamental dagger – baseball bats, broken and sharpened billiard cues, rubber coshes taped together, long wooden sticks, a piece of scaffolding pole, a hockey stick, a black truncheon, a Casco baton, an umbrella with a potentially lethal sharpened end, a smoke canister, a cannabis plant, flags, incriminating notebooks, photograph albums, newspaper cuttings and clothing to aid identification. One photograph actually showed a youth being hit on the head with a hammer, and we found others of the attack by Zulu Warriors on the Australian Bar in Hurst Street on the day of the riot at St Andrew's with Leeds United in May 1985. We were to later charge two of our targets with affray at the Australian Bar because of this evidence. One photograph showed a posing youth holding up his shirt to reveal a knife wound to his back, and another photograph showed a Zulu Warriors flag being raised by supporters on the terraces, whilst others showed injured police officers who had been attacked. Yet more photos, discovered much later than the actual events, showed Francis and Checkers on the pitch during the 'Leeds Riot' of 1985; they went unidentified at the time and thus had not been arrested for that.

Great emphasis was laid by the media on the recovery of a large machete. Photos and images featured the machete being held firmly in the hands of the ACC (Operations) accompanied by the quote, 'These are just people who like hitting other people... It is an operation that needed to be done for the sake of public tranquillity and for the good of football.' This was the graphic message given to the public in relation to these 'potentially death-dealing weapons'. The reality is that knives were the preferred option of the thugs, together with pieces of rubber taped together to make improvised coshes, and telescopic truncheons purchased from abroad. Stanley knives did not appear very common at this stage; they arrived later, and with a vengeance. Rival hooligans would frequently slash people through their clothing, inflicting deep tissue wounds which looked almost like paper cuts but in fact caused fast, dangerous blood flow and severe pain to the victim.

In another interview, the ACC said, 'The amount of evidence that has been gathered during the course of this operation has been quite considerable. That is why I am fairly confident that this will result in convictions at court.' And in yet another interview, a reporter asked him how close we were to 'breaking the back' of the Zulu Warriors. He responded, 'I think that it has been a very successful operation but I think it is dangerous talking about breaking the back or defeating it as it could look like a challenge. I am delighted that we have been able to deal with this operation in the way we have and am feeling rather pleased about it. I am however not issuing challenges for other people to take us on.' He was of course absolutely right to take this approach.

We had known for some time that the Zulus had their own unofficial photographer who revelled in taking real time pictures of disorder. He was Shirt Out, a twenty-two-year-old machine operator from Rubery who liked to absorb the atmosphere of violence but didn't want to get his hands dirty, so to speak. A television reporter joined the arrest team for this individual and travelled with them in a police transit van to his home address. You never quite knew what to expect when you turned up at someone's door and whether it would be a violent confrontation or a non-event. Either way, that team was going to do its job and if necessary force would be met with force, there was only ever going to be one outcome and that was with the criminal having a cell door closed on them. On arrival at the address, the reporter stood back and watched. In his own words: 'The house was surrounded. The suspect lives at the address with his mother and sister. A knock at the door and the police begin their investigations. Each room is searched for evidence. Forty minutes after entry, the officers inspect a red car parked at the front of the house. Inside the vehicle they find photograph albums. Albums packed with graphic photographs of violence taken by the suspect...'

A number of albums containing photographs and press cuttings were recovered from the boot of his vehicle. The television crew was present precisely as the discovery was made, and on film is one of our officers saying to a colleague, 'Bingo, Bryan – we found them!' We had indeed found a full house; it was a great result.

At another address, officers recovered two notebooks containing handwritten details of gang incidents and reference to fans attacking the police and rampaging through various crowded streets across the UK. The books also contained detailed sketches of away football grounds. This gang historian – the Diary Man – nicknamed by us as Oburn, was a twenty-one-year-old polytechnic student with young looks and a big mop of hair. Described in one newspaper as a 'high flying University student from Shirley' who was looking for a career as a systems analyst, he presented no great physical threat to anyone but his particular focus on intelligence gathering gave another sinister dimension to the group's activities. His notebooks contained descriptions of grounds and terraces, modes of travel, and chants, words and songs used by the crowd as well as their mood, and the number of Zulus present; Birmingham City's regular away support had almost doubled in size in 1987 compared to the previous season, from 250 to around 500. He also described police numbers and tactics and incidents of disorder. He was a regular traveller by train to away games and, significantly, in his notes he also described how he had committed wanton criminal damage on trains by smashing lights, roller towels and blinds, and on one occasion pulled the communication cord. The following samples of his 'work' were subsequently entered as evidence in court:

Aston Villa v Birmingham on 7th September 1985 – Kick-off 3pm Division One. After the game walked back to the city centre with hundreds of Blues fans. Didn't see any Villa fans on the way back except a few small groups. No bother. When we got to the junction with Heeley Street and St Andrew's Street everybody started running across the grass chanting 'Zulu'. Then we stopped and regrouped. Then started bricking police horses. One in the middle of the road at Lower Dartmouth Street with people bricking it from all sides. The horse panicked and started charging at people and order was restored... Walked quietly for a while in to the city and on in to John Bright Street. The police on foot and on horses followed us all the way. Hundreds of Blues fans. We turned left into Station Street straight across Hill Street, stopping all the traffic including a WMPTE bus. Now a police car was following us down Station Street. Then just like after West Ham everyone ran through the Midland Red Bus Station through the doors to the Indoor Market. But this time a policeman followed us in so everyone panicked a bit as he tried to arrest people. More police were stationed to the doors of the outside market. About thirty of us went through here and were split from the rest. We went up the circular ramp back into the Bull Ring but police were waiting at the doors and followed us out. Many of the others were now in the outdoor market and we grouped up again. About 100 or so Blues fans. Then we ran across the Bull Ring by St Martins Circus Queensway stopping traffic to the subway outside Moor Street. Only one copper on foot followed us and he jumped over a wall to stop us as we went into the subway. Then a police van arrived pulling up behind us at the entrance to the subway and we were effectively trapped. Everybody panicked. Some carried on through the subway some went back past the van. The police piled out of the van and arrested at least one fan. One put a struggle up and dragged a copper to the ground. He stayed lying there. A police motorcyclist had also arrived now and some bricks were thrown from near the entrance to Moor Street Station at the police van. But the crowd had now dispersed. Not long after there was a major fight between Blues and Villa fans at Lancaster Circus Fire Station with horses used to split the crowd who threw concrete some serious injuries and arrests.

And from the following year but the same football season:

West Bromwich Albion v Birmingham on 8th February 1986 – Kick-off 3pm Division One. Main stand mostly full although gaps towards corner each end block only. Executive club now virtually full. Just half a dozen or so empty seats in the back rows nearer Railway End. Paddocks mainly empty as usual. City stand full in centre though gaps towards back and mainly empty in the wings. No blues fans allowed in Tilton. Corner nearly empty plus gaps at front of Kop. Mostly full at back of

Kop although pushing and shoving led to gap forming at back during game which filled up again later. About 1500 WBA fans quite well filled anyway although there were large gaps at front and towards corner and not that packed over most of the enclosure. A few hundred at most in seats towards corner of main stand. Quiet almost throughout game although you could just about hear faint singing near end and they were clapping rapturously at final whistle. Blues fans didn't seem very interested in the game. The Kop were singing silly songs like 'Brum Brum Brum' after only a few minutes and even though the team were putting some good moves together nobody was really shouting them on. Singing was loud at times from the back of the Kop but the fans' hearts didn't really seem to be in it. Several hundred walked into town after. We could see the WBA fans coming down Garrison Lane as we walked down Lower Dartmouth Street but the police kept us apart at the island with horses. The Albion fans were escorted up Lawley Street, and the Blues fans up Great Barr Street and Fazeley Street into town. There was no real bother on the way and the police were fairly low profile although there were several vans including the Hoolivan and horses. The Blues fans were spread out and stretched back for quite a long way. An ambulance followed us along. When we got to the bridge over Fazeley Street we started singing underneath it. There were some people on top of the bridge looking over at us and plenty of people about in town shopping. We were singing 'Birmingham' and 'We love you City'. Then everyone started running up Albert Street towards High Street chanting. Police chasing us on foot with dogs and on horses. Everyone was now all over *the street with police struggling to gain control and ordinary people running to get out of the way. It calmed down and about fifty to a hundred of us then walked up Union Street which is pedestrianised, singing 'We hate Villa and we hate Villa'. Lots of ordinary shoppers in the street. Police stopped us at Corporation Street and they made us walk down the street as we were singing 'We love you City'. We went up the ramp into the station. Soon kicked out of main doors of station walked down side down car park ramp and up Navigation Street and Stephenson Street and back onto the ramp in New Street. Here a load of WBA were coming up the ramp as well as Blues and no one knew who was who. The police seemed to think we were all Albion fans and made us all go down the steps into Stephenson Street where the WBA fans got their buses. Here the Blues fans, a hundred of us, charged at Albion fans with a fight and police running behind to catch up. Everyone ran into Navigation Street and the police then escorted us on foot. An ambulance came past with an Albion fan presum- ably. We went down John Bright Street then first left onto Hill Street up the car park ramp towards the station again. Blues fans now on both sides of the road with coppers following on foot. Not many of us. Copper on motorcycle followed us up the ramp and parked across it grabbing people and trying to stop them getting past. He failed and we went back into New Street Station. Trouble virtually over by now though. A few of us came back out of the station and hung around the car park for a while then went over to the outside steps and looked over the wall overlooking Station Street. Four horses went past and one Zulu with us threw something and hit one copper on the head. Immediately another horse came up the car park ramp after us and we all ran up the steps back into the Birmingham Shopping Centre chanting 'Zulu'. Went back into the station but quiet by now and soon went home.*

He also wrote of avoiding paying for tickets as well as routinely confronting the police. It was interesting that he always referred to the gang as 'the Zulus' and thus as something of a separate entity, as if he was not involved but was detached from them. Whilst it was clear that he was not part of the hardcore group, it was also clear that he routinely attached himself to them and was comfortable in actually taking on the mantle of a Zulu when in these group situations. All the time he had been playing with fire and was finally going to get his fingers burnt. It was quite simply a way of life for him and one which he appeared to relish. Whilst he clearly had some interest in the outcome of football matches he had a clear focus too on violence, relishing being and feeling a part of it. He was far from a passive observer.

At one target's address in Chelmsley Wood, a number of the hooligans' calling cards were recovered. One adapted version had the innocent details of Birmingham City Clubcall on one side but on the other was the message 'Zulu Warriors Pride of the Midlands' with a picture of a person with the head of a bulldog piercing the chest of a lion with a blood-stained spear. Other calling cards had previously been found declaring 'You have been Zapped by a Zulu'.

*

No complaints were made against the police by any of our targets during the course of Red Card and no problems arose over the correct execution of the search warrants. Although it was necessary to force entry to property in two cases, the occupants did not put up any physical resistance. I think that most of the individuals we visited were simply in shock. There were subsequently no disputes over identification either. During the course of their police interviews, suspects were initially shown sections of video footage or photographs and were invited to confirm that it was them in the pictures; the images did not show them doing anything unlawful. They were then shown sections where there was primary evidence which linked them to crimes – and then they were invited to re-confirm that it was them in the pictures. This approach usually deflated the suspect, as the realisation that they were looking at irrefutable and damning evidence sank in. When faced with the visual evidence, nearly all of the defendants made admissions in varying degrees; only one made a total denial of everything put to him. Most of those arrested were in some form of employment, ranging from government work schemes through to manual labour. More than half of them had previous convictions. A disproportionate number resided in the E Division area of the force, as had been expected.

The vast majority of those arrested in the first of the co-ordinated phases spent a night in the cells before appearing before a special court at Birmingham Magistrates Court on 8 October. They were charged with offences including conspiracy to commit public order offences, wounding, violent disorder and other matters. Shortly before the court proceedings, they were transferred to the Central Lock Up at Steelhouse Lane Police Station and placed in holding cells beneath the courts. They would, one by one, soon be climbing the steps into the dock, to be dealt with in batches.

When it came to the stabbing of the Tottenham youth on Hill Street, the Crown Prosecution Service considered an indictment for an offence of riot in the first instance, which would have required the consent of the Director of Public Prosecutions. One prominent, nineteen-year-old Junior Business Boy from the Chelmsley Wood area was sent to prison for nine months for his part in this offence and an unrelated offence of wounding. Whilst on bail awaiting trial, he failed a condition of his bail terms of reporting in to his local police station during the Christmas period but he was let off by the court on the basis that his father said he had been at home, ill in bed!

The court's public gallery was packed with relatives and friends of the accused men, and was heavily guarded by police officers. The hearing itself was presided over by Stipendiary Magistrate William Probert. The court buildings were imposing, the appropriate intention no doubt, in Victorian style. Wood panelling is prevalent in the court rooms, reinforcing the sense of gravitas and protocol demanding respect. When the Stipendiary Magistrate spoke, which ever 'side' you were on, you made a noise at your peril. That day, twenty-one defendants were remanded in custody for seven days to prison. Two, including our main target from the Hill Street incident, were remanded to police cells for twenty-four hours to enable further interviews to take place. Those who were eventually granted bail had strict conditions imposed on them while they were on bail; these included not to go within one mile of any Football League club ground in the country, to refrain from entering Birmingham city centre as defined by the Inner Ring Road (unless to see a solicitor or attend court) and to report at police stations at 3.30 p.m. every Saturday. They were some of the most stringent bail conditions I have seen throughout my service, proving to be very effective in curtailing the defendants' criminal activities and association.

Those suspects who were granted bail were allowed to leave the court. Their ordeal, however, was not over, as the press were waiting for them outside. This caused some of the suspects to hide their faces to try and avoid being photographed; they didn't appear so proud of their actions now.

CHAPTER 14

FINAL SCORE

OPERATION RED CARD ran from January to October 1987, during the course of which sixty-seven men and youths were arrested for a range of crimes, most of them involving serious violence. Following the arrests of the main offenders, twenty-four prosecution files were prepared for the Crown Prosecution Service, the biggest of which related to the twenty-seven defendants implicated in the Hill Street stabbing, which contained one hundred and thirteen witness statements. We submitted all of the prosecution evidence to the CPS by January 1988, the speed of which was something of an achievement in itself. The main defendants were then committed to trial at the Crown Court in March 1988, also in notably fast-track style.

On 1 March, the Birmingham Evening Mail reported, 'A total of ninety-five young men were due to appear before Birmingham Magistrates today in one of the city's biggest court crackdowns on alleged soccer hooligans. A batch of forty-five people arrested during police raids code-named "Operation Red Card" were due to face charges relating to organised violence at Birmingham City matches. And a further 50 Birmingham and Nottingham fans were due before the Court in relation to violence at the Birmingham City against Nottingham Forrest FA Cup tie on February 20th 1988. Police filmed much of the crowd trouble at the cup tie at St Andrew's with video recorders and recorded evidence will be available for use as prosecution evidence.'

The first twenty-six Red Card defendants were committed for trial under Section Two of the 1986 Public Order Act, charged with using and threatening violence in Hill Street, Birmingham, on 11 April 1987. One of them, our target Mini Driver, was remanded in custody. The remainder were granted bail until their trial at Crown Court with strict conditions imposed.

It certainly felt like the battle was being taken to the hooligans now, but there was never any room for complacency. That same month, PC Neil Cook suffered a cut eye when 'headbutted in the face in a Birmingham police station by a man arrested after apparently being turned away from St Andrew's Football Ground,' according to the Evening Mail. PC Cook had been on duty at the Birmingham City versus West Bromwich Albion match when summoned to deal with a gang of men who were believed to have damaged a vehicle after having been turned away from the match. Five men were taken to Stechford Police Station for questioning but as they entered the police yard a fight broke out and the officer was injured.

As hooliganism seemed to be a permanent blight on football, the constant issue of money and funding grew in significance with it. It was announced on 31 March that police charges to West Midlands soccer clubs for football duties were to double for the next year. The six clubs would be ordered to pay almost £500,000 for police at home games, a one hundred per cent increase. This would almost certainly mean the clubs would increase their admission charges for spectators, a clear sign that the yobs were harming the game in more ways than had perhaps been considered. Birmingham MP Denis Howell planned to protest to the Home Secretary, saying, 'We strongly object to having to pay for protection which should be ours of right.' It was said that Birmingham City's contribution would increase from £47,000 to nearly £77,000 per match, and councillor Mick Ablett, the Police Authority chairman, said that even this increase would not meet the total cost of football policing in the area, which was more than £750,000.

Of course, our efforts had not gone unnoticed by other forces. On 30 October, I briefed the divisional chief superintendent on the G Division, based at Wolverhampton, and outlined the tactics we had used. Wolverhampton Wanderers had their own serious problems with a violent element and their police brass were determined to do something about it. Elven days later, I briefed a team of G Division officers who were involved in what they named Operation GROWTH, an acronym for Get Rid Of Wolverhampton's Troublesome Hooligans. I was delighted to be able to help. I had developed a taste for large-scale, set-piece operations and continued to try to come up with new initiatives with that in mind.

In the spring of 1988, we were having new problems with robberies in Birmingham city centre. We knew who some of the offenders were but not all of them and we needed to find a way to stop the flow of offences. What we were more sure about was that most of them travelled into the city by bus. An idea was forming. In 1920s Chicago, when the Prohibition agent Eliot Ness was struggling to prove gangster Al Capone was guilty of numerous violent crimes as well violating Prohibition laws, he famously went for him via another route, choosing to pursue him for tax evasion, a lesser charge but the scheme worked perfectly and Capone was sentenced, I believe, to eleven years' imprisonment. Using similar thinking, if we couldn't get these Birmingham thieves for robbery then we would have to find other ways of disrupting them.

Thus Operation Buzz was born. I oversaw it while still in the local intelligence role. And in March 1988, after working with West Midlands Travel revenue protection inspectors, British Transport Police, and OSU officers, we arrested eighteen people for a variety of offences including theft, fraud and possessing drugs. During a three-day follow-up operation in April, over 3,000 buses entering the city centre were checked by fifteen revenue inspectors and forty police officers, many of whom were again from the OSU. Ninety-two pre-paid travel cards and tickets were seized for being either forged, stolen, or fraudulently altered, and fifty people were arrested for offences ranging from fraud, deception, robbery and assault to possessing offensive weapons and drugs. There were literally queues of officers and prisoners waiting to go into the Central Lockup at Steelhouse Lane to be processed, and although the personnel had been warned about the possible increase in workload, I wasn't particularly popular with the custody staff, as they were now so busy. 'What the fuck is all this lot about? As if we don't have enough to do,' would come the comments but I was still enjoying the job and used to receiving flak, even though it occasionally came from my own side! I maintained my personal ethos that we would take out the roots and as many branches as we could – the more the better. It was designed to be a shock tactic and it worked.

In May 1988, Operation Red Card hit the media headlines again following the collapse of three undercover football operations in the Metropolitan Police area. Conspiracy charges against five Millwall fans during the course of Operation Dirty Den, an undercover infiltration of the club's hooligan fraternity, were dropped after the prosecution offered no evidence at the trial at Southwark Crown Court. Four of the Millwall followers still faced charges of affray, brought by the BTP, but overall the dropped charges were a serious blow to this type of operation and damaged public confidence in such tactics.

LIAM: The Millwall guy I arrested at West Brom [during season 1986–87] was one of the defendants in the Millwall undercover operation and I had to go to Southwark Crown Court to give evidence, as they used my arrest as part of the conspiracy evidence. I was in the witness box for two hours. The defence accepted my evidence as the guy had previously pleaded guilty to my arrest but they kept going on about the plans of the ground and asking me to go over again and again where I had made my arrest. They said that the evidence from the Metropolitan Police undercover officers could not be right because where they had marked him as being in the ground was the home end and not the away end where I had made the arrest. They were acquitted.

The Millwall case collapsed within two weeks of two other trials failing, involving West Ham fans at Snaresbrook Crown Court and Chelsea fans at Knightsbridge Crown Court.

Notwithstanding those failures, we were highly confident that there were no weaknesses or mistakes in our operation. We had worked tirelessly to ensure that everything was correct and incontrovertible, and the then-Chief Constable of West Midlands Police, (now Sir) Geoffrey Dear, agreed, saying that he was satisfied with the way evidence was gathered in Red Card as well as in Operation GROWTH, the Wolverhampton investigation which followed on soon after ours was curtailed. 'We are confident the prosecutions will continue to run,' he said. 'The evidence was gained in a totally different way to the Metropolitan Police cases.' Of course, I was very glad of the fact that I had taken the opportunity of looking at the approach taken by the Metropolitan Police in respect of their operations before we started our own. We learned valuable lessons throughout, especially in terms of being able to corroborate evidence provided from undercover sources. In hindsight, it seems we adhered to the correct procedures more than those other operations had. On the flipside of my confidence though was the knowledge that I was ultimately accountable if anything went wrong with our operation. Thankfully, nothing did go wrong and, interestingly here, the judge presiding in court told journalists they could report 'anything that has taken place in this court today'.

The quality of our operation's evidence was such that ultimately it would not be necessary for any full trials to take place. A full trial is one where the defendants plead not guilty, therefore requiring witnesses to give evidence from the box to the judge and jury, before then being cross-examined by the defence barrister. In a guilty plea hearing, witnesses are not required to give evidence, as the circumstances are outlined by the prosecuting barrister, who might read out some of the witness statements and summarise the case before the defence barrister offers mitigation. None of the witnesses, and none of the officers who had been deployed covertly, would be required to give evidence, thus taking a great deal of pressure off them while leaving the defendants still trying to guess the identities of the coverts (which all explains why some of the names in this book have been changed – to protect the innocent). I occasionally attended both the magistrates' and the Crown Court proceedings, standing with colleagues amongst some of the defendants waiting to be dealt with. I remained anonymous and they had no idea what role I had played in the whole affair. Had they known me, there might well have been a problem or two, but regardless, I certainly felt no sympathy for them.

Twelve of our main target group faced an indictment for conspiracy to fight, display force, and thereby make an affray or affrays, for the period between 1 January 1985 and 31 March 1987, and three of them faced a specific historical charge in relation to affray at St Andrew's during the match with Leeds United on 11 May 1985. In the end, the bulk of the defendants pleaded guilty to offences where there was additional visual evidence to support the cases against them. Sixteen defendants subsequently received immediate custodial sentences of varying lengths, and seven received suspended sentences. Twenty-four were fined and eleven were bound over to keep the peace or were given probation orders or conditional discharges. Two cases were discontinued by the CPS and the remainder of the suspects were interviewed on arrest but not charged.

Steve Trenbirth remembered vividly being in Crown Court for the first plea and directions, and thinking he had never seen so many wigs and barristers in one room before. 'Plea and directions' is a technical phrase to describe a sequence of events in court. For instance, it might mean remanding a case for two to three weeks following a guilty plea if there is a likelihood of a custodial sentence, as this could allow for social inquiry or probation reports to be prepared or character witnesses to be called. Alternatively, in the case of a not guilty plea it might be about setting a date for a trial and estimating its length as well as co-ordinating court attendance of witnesses and so on. The wigs and barristers were all worried about the hefty prison sentences that had been given in the recent Chelsea trial, so most of our defendants started by entering 'not guilty' pleas. A few would plead guilty though, and later, when the barristers saw how lenient the sentencing was, there was a lot of scurrying round by the legal profession, with defendants being brought back into court to ask for the charges to be put to them again so that they could change their plea to guilty.

Many people over the years have tried to analyse and define what a football hooligan is and why they behave as they do. Prosecuting QC Brian Escott Cox referred at Birmingham

Crown Court to the fact that the accused had engaged in the Hill Street incident 'without any thought for terrified shoppers who were caught in the crossfire'. He added, 'Their motivation is not to be excused, as in civil disturbances where people have been motivated by religious, political, or financial necessity, this was lust for violence for its own sake.'

On November 17, in sentencing one of the main offenders, Judge Richard Toyn said, 'Your degree of involvement and pride in it is demonstrated by your observation to police officers that you and your colleagues had your reputation to uphold.' This target normally wore gold-rimmed spectacles and looked quite studious. He even wore them when fighting. We nicknamed him Milk Race. 'Whether any of them are members of a defined group called the Zulus or Zulu Warriors is immaterial, they have pursued violence against other groups, and the enthusiasts looking forward with eager anticipation to fighting with other fans at grounds and in public streets,' the judge later added. 'Sadly, indeed tragically, many of the young men concerned are of hitherto good character and some were of excellent educational attainment. The barbarism displayed by such intelligent young people is both astounding and depressing.'

Not everyone was happy with the outcome. Following what were perceived by many to be relatively light sentences, politics entered the arena with comments from two local members of Parliament. 'The bovver boys who plague our football grounds will be laughing at these totally inadequate sentences,' said Yardley MP David Gilroy Bevan. 'These criminals and thugs have contributed to the decline of Birmingham

City. Unless the punishment can be made to fit the crime, the club stands little chance of attracting decent law-abiding families.' Selly Oak Conservative MP Anthony Beaumont-Dark also weighed in, saying, 'The judge has let down police officers... The ringleaders should have been sent down for at least five years to act as an example to Britain's soccer louts. They are a disease on our society.'

Personally, I chose to try and ignore the debate about the sentencing, as throughout my police service I believed it to be better to separate policing outcomes from judicial ones. A police officer cannot afford to feel disappointment, otherwise they risk losing their edge. The primary objective for us is to do our best in our jobs and to let others get on with theirs. Once you start to ask yourself what the point of it all is because the criminals won't receive enough punishment, you become a poorer investigator. Your own work suffers and thus so does your attitude and approach to life.

Speaking at the end of the main court cases, my divisional chief superintendent, who later went on to become the Deputy Chief Constable of West Midlands Police, said, 'The result is a success and it has vindicated the kind of operation which led to the trial. The difference between this case and the operations in London was the use of recordings of thuggery made on video tape...' Caroline Gall's Zulus stated that several prominent members of the gang luckily escaped the Operation Red Card dragnet, with 'Cud' away on holiday when the raids were carried out and 'Wally' resident in prison in Exeter serving a nine-month term. Perhaps Wally was the individual signing his prison letters 'The Guvenor'.

In summary, the final, and to our mind impressive, 'scores', including the clothing descriptions we used for each defendant, were as follows:

1. Francis. Our main target, the leader. Of West Indian origin, twenty-one years of age, stocky build, short tight curly hair, living in Washwood Heath, Birmingham. Clothing: grey/black horizontal striped jacket or black loose-fit jacket, blue V-neck top with yellow piping. Brown shoes. Sentenced to eighteen months in prison.

2. Green Hood. A second lieutenant always close to target 1. White male, aged twenty-two, from Hodge Hill, Birmingham. Stocky build, fat face, short haircut. Green cotton cagoule with hood pulled tightly around the face (whatever the weather conditions) and white rectangular patch on the left arm. Sometimes wore a white baseball cap, jeans and trainers, or round-neck jumper with a big face design on the left side. A smoker, he worked as a beader. Imprisoned for a total of fifteen months.

3. Milk Race. Another second lieutenant close to Cab and the leader Francis. West Indian origin, nineteen years of age, slim build, from Bordesley Green. Had short black curly hair and also had a bit of a moustache. Wore white, Milk Race cycling cap, with dark blue tracksuit with white piping on the legs, also a brown leather jacket and large, gold-rimmed spectacles. An electrician by trade. Received twenty-one months' imprisonment.

4. Second Out. Nickname derived from his being the second out of The Crown pub when the Tottenham fight was

about to explode. Very little information on him other than he was a light-skinned West Indian wearing a grey jacket with a white collar.

5. Raincoat. Involved in arranging the fight at Hill Street. West Indian male, twenty-one years old, short in height, short black styled hair, from Warstock, Birmingham. Cream coloured raincoat. Employed as an assistant cook. Received a six-month sentence.

6. Mini Driver. Driver of the Mini car which was used to take the fight arrangers to meet their Tottenham counterparts before the events on Hill Street. White male, aged nineteen, from Ladywood, Birmingham. Curly hair and a thin moustache. Black leather bomber jacket, black crewneck jumper, a gold necklace with encrusted stones on it. Received a prison sentence.

7. Wimpy. Was definitely one that 'got away' due to our not being able to confirm his identity or sufficient personal data to enable us to arrest him.

8. Sidekick. Involved in the Hill Street events. White, twenty, from Ward End in Birmingham. Clean shaven and with collar-length hair. Wore a dark leather zip-up bomber jacket or beige, full-length, belted raincoat. Employed as a flower seller. Subsequently fined and also received a suspended prison sentence for a number of public order offences.

9. Red. Believed to be heavily involved in the incidents at The Fox pub involving Portsmouth followers in March 1987. Male of Asian appearance, twenty-one years of age, from Bordesley Green. Wore a red jumper, hence the nickname. Sent to prison.

10. Elm. White youth, seventeen, from Sheldon, Birmingham. Slim and tall, he had short brown hair with a centre parting. Green, waxed, three-quarter-length jacket or denim jacket, brown shirt, blue jeans. Fined for violent disorder at Hill Street during the Tottenham incidents.

11. Fat Ginger. Another unknown target present at Hill Street. White male, wore a peach coloured V-neck jumper, blue tracksuit bottoms with white vertical stripes. Gold earring in his left ear.

12. Orange. In attendance at Hill Street. Of Asian appearance, seventeen years of age, from Bordesley Green. Slim build, a moustache. Orange jumper with 'D Interet' on it. Fined.

13. Checkers. Hill Street involvement. Of 'mixed race' appearance (the terminology used then),, male, twenty years of age, from Bordesley Green. Unemployed, had skinhead-style black hair. Long-sleeved woollen shirt/cardigan, blue and green with large checks. Bound over to keep the peace for two years.

14. Cab. The target who was convicted for wounding at The Swan pub; he was also present during the Hill Street mayhem. West Indian male, twenty, from Bordesley Green. Medium black curly hair, big eyebrows and a slight moustache. He was medium build and a known shoplifter. Green padded anorak with mustard coloured lining in the hood. Outwardly quiet but clearly not afraid of anyone, he possessed a deep-seated mistrust and dislike of the police.

15. Bro. Involved in the Hill Street events. Light-skinned West Indian male, twenty-three, from Nechells in Birmingham.

Short afro-style haircut and a small goatee beard. Dark coloured, zip-up leather jacket. Bound over to keep the peace for two years.

16. Bumble. Hill Street involvement. Unknown target. White male wearing a two-tone, orange-ringed jumper.

17. Saint. Guilty of Hill Street involvement. West Indian male, eighteen, from Longbridge in Birmingham. Clean shaven with short black curly hair. Fined for threatening behaviour.

18. Fats. Well known shoplifter with a large waistline. Came from the Bordesley Green area, West Indian origin, age 21 years. He received a suspended prison sentence.

19. Michael. West Indian origin, aged nineteen, from Chelmsley Wood. Sentenced to nine months in prison.

20. Woody. White male, nineteen, from Edgbaston. Nine months in prison.

21. Shirt Out. Also known to be the Zulu Warriors' photographer. White male, twenty-two, from Rubery in Birmingham. Slim build. Baseball cap with studs in, green jacket with red/white patches. A low-key character but his camera ensured important participation in some of the gang's activities. He eventually received a fine and a suspended prison sentence, with the judge commenting, 'You have the curious position of being the photographer. You didn't get involved, but you did take a childish and inane delight in being there.'

22. Yellow Top. White male, wore a bright yellow jumper when first witnessed. At the Hill Street fight but ultimately he stayed unidentified.

23. Pint Pot. Also a white male, present at the Hill Street fight and not identified.

24. Light. Was also witnessed at Hill Street. Light-skinned West Indian male, nineteen, from Oldbury in the West Midlands. Black Barbour jacket or leather hooded jacket. Sentenced to fifteen months' imprisonment for violent disorder.

25. Hoop. Hill Street attendance also. Light-skinned West Indian male, twenty-one, from Druids Heath, Birmingham. An electrician. Short curly black hair, with slight moustache. Red sweatshirt and blue jacket. Later fined for violent disorder.

26. Midwest. At Hill Street. West Indian male, nineteen. From Lozells, Birmingham. Wearing a T-shirt with the motif 'Midwest State College'. Red baseball cap, or blue/white baseball cap. Fined for violent disorder.

27. Spike Blond. Another white male who was present at the Hill Street fight but remained unidentified.

28. Grease Head. Was at Hill Street. White male, twenty-two, from Kings Norton, Birmingham. Clean-cut appearance. Black leather jacket. Fined for violent disorder.

29. Turn Up. Also witnessed at Hill Street. West Indian male, eighteen, from Sparkbrook, Birmingham. Short black curly hair and large ears. Blue jeans turned up at the bottom and 'Aviator' sweatshirt. Decorator. Sentenced to three years' probation.

30. Sightseer. Twenty-three years old, from Cannock. Refused the charge against him. No further action. 'Refuse charge' is a technical term to indicate that the evidence has been

considered by someone such as a custody officer, a senior police officer or even a prosecuting solicitor and a decision made not to formally charge the prisoner with an offence. The decision is normally made on the basis that there is insufficient evidence to proceed, or in some cases it is not in the public interest to do so; for example, in the case of a vulnerable or elderly person stealing a very small amount of property. Clearly that did not apply to Operation Red Card's suspects but the bar has always been set quite high to meet standards of evidence which are sufficient to initiate court proceedings with. If in doubt, the accused normally benefited. It was not a decision for the accused to be involved in: if charged the details would be read out to them, and they would be invited to reply, under caution, and provided with a copy of the charge sheet. There is a distinction to be made between having sufficient grounds to arrest someone by way of the information available and having sufficient evidence with which to formally charge someone with an offence.

31. Wax. Also part of the Hill Street incidents. White male, twenty-one, from Northfield, Birmingham. Green, three-quarter-length wax jacket. Sentenced to six months' imprisonment for violent disorder.

32. Style. At Hill Street, white male, nineteen, from Hodge Hill, Birmingham. He worked as a warehouseman. Clean shaven, with a mop of ginger hair with a side parting. Received a fine. Bail conditions varied whilst he had a holiday in Tenerife and a trip to Jersey.

33. Racer. At Hill Street. Nineteen, from Quinton in

Birmingham. Sentenced to six months in prison for violent disorder.

34. Frank. Arrested for fighting on the day Portsmouth FC were the visitors to St Andrew's. Court result unconfirmed.

35. Brown Jacket. White male, at the Hill Street disorder but not identified.

36. Fossil. At Hill Street. Not a hardcore Zulu Warrior, more of a hard drinker who played a 'supporting' role. White, aged thirty, from Chelmsley Wood. A caretaker, stocky build. Bound over to keep the peace for two years.

37. Wise. Taken into custody but later released without charge.

38. Stone. Involved in events at the Stoke City game. White male, twenty-two, from Bromford in Birmingham. Sent to prison for six months.

39. Yellow Hood. West Indian male, another target who was recorded as being at Hill Street but who remained unidentified.

40. Meatloaf. West Indian male, thirty-two, from Bordesley Green. Was taken to Digbeth Police Station and interviewed regarding an offence of criminal damage at Aston Villa football ground for which no further action was taken. However, he was also dealt with for an outstanding-fine commitment warrant to prison and thus kept in custody.

41. Harry. Was known to have Zulu connections and frequented The Crown. White male, twenty-nine, short hair going bald on top and was generally unshaven. From

Lozells in Birmingham. Case for violent disorder discontinued due to appearance at court for other matters.

42. Blue Boy. White Male. Wearing a blue jumper while present at Hill Street but was not identified.

43. Gingerbeard. Admitted to being present at Hill Street. White, bearded twenty-seven-year-old from Castle Bromwich. Wore jeans and T-shirts. Employed as a decorator. Bound over to keep the peace for two years.

44. Short Ginger. Was involved in the Hill Street events. White male, eighteen, from West Heath in Birmingham. Stocky build, short ginger hair and a slight moustache. Received a fine.

45. Specs. At Hill Street. White male, thirty, a civil servant from Solihull. Wore blue-framed spectacles. Short in height, clean shaven and of generally neat appearance. Bound over to keep the peace for two years.

46. Rooky. Twenty-year-old from Castle Bromwich. Fined and received a twelve-month suspended prison sentence.

47. Bruno. 'Mixed race', aged twenty, from Bordesley Green. Fined.

48. Sleepy. Involved with incidents at Werneth Railway Station near to Oldham Athletic FC. Asian male, thirty, from Sparkbrook. Black hair and slight moustache. Received a fine.

49. Dal. White male, aged twenty-five, from Lea Village. Fined.

50. Sharp. B Team member, white, nineteen, from Streetly, West Midlands. Long straight hair with a fringe over his left eye. Slim build. Fawn-coloured leather jacket. A

factory worker. Fined for offences at Hull and Stoke City games.

51. Goofy. Another B Team member, white, twenty-one, from Redditch in Worcestershire. Slim build, clean shaven, narrow face, slightly protruding teeth. Deerstalker hat and blue/red ski jacket. He was employed as a labourer. Later went to prison for seven months.

52. Baby Face. B Team member and brother of target number 51, Goofy. White, aged seventeen, from Redditch. Employed as a factory worker. Very young-looking face, short brown hair, big ears. Fined.

53. Benetton. B Team member. Ginger, curly-haired white male, twenty-one, from Kitts Green in Birmingham. A pink Benetton jumper, generally scruffy appearance. He was fined for involvement in the Hull City incident at St Andrew's where a planned, collective assault on one of our police inspectors looked imminent.

54. Dek. B Team member, white male, twenty-two, from Small Heath. Allowed to get married a week after being arrested. Dark brown hair with moustache. Later fined for a public order offence at the Shrewsbury Town game.

55. Grace. B Team member. West Indian male, twenty, from Yardley Wood in Birmingham. Short afro haircut with moustache. Green jumper, brown moccasin shoes. Fined for the Hull events for unlawful assembly.

56. Comedian. B Team member, white male, nineteen, from Yardley Wood, Birmingham. Yellow jumper. Opened carriage doors whilst train was in motion, charged with endangering safety of passengers. Fined.

57. Baseball Cap. B Team member, white male, twenty, from Northfield. Short in height with cropped hair and clean-shaven face. Black baseball cap and black leather jacket. Received a suspended prison sentence for offences at the Hull match.

58. Oburn. Was also the Diary Man as well as the gang's historian. Jailed for six months.

59. West. A twenty-four-year-old from Lichfield. He was fined for public order violations.

60. Smart Blond. A white male who was observed at Hill Street but stayed unidentified.

61. Frown. Also at Hill Street. West Indian male, nineteen, from Quinton. Short curly black hair, he always seemed to be frowning. Fined for violent disorder.

62. Mop. Also at the Stoke game. A B Team member, white, nineteen, from Kitts Green, employed as a bed maker. Straggly black hair, collar length, and had a moustache. Narrow features. Bound over for two years to keep the peace.

63. Ant. Went to prison for twenty-eight days for theft.

64. Charlie. Received two years' probation for theft.

65. Abbey. Arrested for receiving stolen property. Suspended prison sentence.

66. Ken. Receiving stolen property. Conditional discharge of twelve months.

67. Pepper. Also prosecuted for receiving stolen property. Suspended prison sentence.

68. Poet. Receiving stolen property. Twelve-month conditional discharge.

69. Gerry. Receiving stolen property; case discontinued.

70. Fife. Was arrested for criminal damage at The Fox pub in March 1987.

71. Stitch. His real name was not ascertained, and whilst he was an active Zulu he was not arrested in Operation Red Card.

72. Chancer. West Indian male who lived in the Warstock district. Refused charge regarding burglary.

73. Robin. White male, aged twenty-five, from Sutton Coldfield. Was dealt with for a Section 5 (threatening behaviour) on the day of The Fox incident but no further action on other matters.

74. Perry. A twenty-year-old from Quinton who was refused charge.

75. Sheet. Was at Hill Street. White male, twenty-four, from Great Barr, Birmingham. A sheet metal worker, he was bound over to keep the peace for two years. He was granted a bail variation for a holiday in Jersey prior to being dealt with.

Finally, targets 76 to 81 consisted of one black and five white men of varying ages. They were not linked and their cases not proceeded with owing to being bracketed as 'intelligence only'. This refers to our possessing information on a suspect that does not develop into evidence sufficient to charge them with, hence no court proceedings. These targets, in numerical order, were nicknamed Londoner, Swansea Boy, Ron, Tam, Major and Legal.

When we first started the operation we had a lot of names,

and many others were added, but eventually we had to draw the line between intelligence and evidence and inevitably some escaped justice.

*

Operation GROWTH began on 30 November 1987. We shared our experiences with the Wolverhampton officers involved, hoping it would help their cause. GROWTH was aimed very much at the same layers of organised criminality witnessed in Red Card and among other hooligan groups active in the UK. One of its catalysts was the serious disorder when 4,000 Wolverhampton Wanderers supporters had attended an away game at Scarborough that August. The result was what could only be described as carnage. This was coincidentally the same date on which Zulu Warriors were fighting with Stoke fans in Birmingham. The Wolves yobs, known as the Subway Army, seemed to like their weekends away, also causing notable disturbances in the coastal resorts of Torquay and Southend.

GROWTH identified some three hundred potential suspects in its early stages, and resulted in a massive series of dawn raids in March 1988, signalling another major blow to the country's football hooligans. More than 250 officers raided sixty-eight homes in a co-ordinated operation targeting Wolverhampton Wanderers thugs, the largest such round-up ever. Those arrested were taken to six police stations across the region. A team of eight policemen had worked undercover for months, posing as hooligans to infiltrate the trouble-makers known as the 'Bridge Boys' after the bridge opposite

Wolverhampton Railway Station, the location of numerous ambushes on opposing fans. One undercover officer was even beaten up by opposing fans at an away game in Exeter but his cuts and bruises served to boost his cover. Seven other officers were engaged on the inquiry full-time. Knives, scrapbooks, calling cards and stolen jewellery taken from a looted shop in Wolverhampton were recovered. More than thirty additional targets remained to be seen in a follow-up phase. Shockingly, it was later confirmed that one of those still under investigation was a police constable from the Black Country, who was captured off duty on video at the scene of a disturbance.

 If anyone still doubts the dangers and challenges of undercover work, here are some recollections kindly provided by a couple of the officers on that operation. They make sobering reading. Their true identities have been protected, for obvious reasons.

COVERT OFFICER STEVE: I had known 'James' since 1981 and knew that he had been working undercover on an operation looking at the Zulu Warriors with Mike Layton, who I also knew quite well. As a BTP officer I was used to dealing with football fans every Saturday and the Zulu Warriors regularly came onto New Street Station after home games. We didn't come across the Zulus on Operation GROWTH because they were in a different division, but in the mid-eighties I was involved in one particularly bad experience with them. We took a train up to Manchester, which had to be stopped at Stockport. The Zulus were rammed in one carriage which they completed wrecked and turned all of the lights out in.

They were beating their feet on the floor and chanting 'Zulu' and challenging us to take them on. There were twelve of us on the train because we expected trouble but there was no point getting into a fight, so we locked them in and took them back to Birmingham. It was like a routine.

I used to be a West Bromwich Albion fan but I lost interest when I joined the police. I knew very little about Wolverhampton Wanderers but when I was approached to do an undercover job on their hooligans I said 'yes' straight away. I was the right age and had a Black Country accent. Those were my qualifications!

After several meetings I started with a number of officers from the West Midlands, plus an officer from West Mercia Police and one from Staffordshire. We met the Operation Red Card team for a briefing and learnt as much as we could from them. One thing was not to have a moustache – it was a giveaway that you were a police officer – and I had an earring put in. I wore an old sheepskin coat which I kept in the garage. They used to call me and my partner 'Steptoe and Son'. By the end of the operation we were the only two who managed to stay together throughout. A number had to leave early because the risks of being exposed as undercover officers became too great.

I remember a particularly scary moment when Cardiff were playing at Wolverhampton and we were in a pub called The George, which was rammed with two to three hundred Wolves hooligans. There was a really nasty atmosphere and suddenly someone shouted that Cardiff fans were outside. We both moved towards the front doors to see what was going on but it was a false alarm. Suddenly we were the centre of attention, with people from Tipton staring at us, making 'pig noises' and saying how bad the room smelt. There was no way out with the doors locked and we had no phones or radios. Things weren't looking good for us. Suddenly a target I knew, who we nick-named Hot Dog because we saw him once trying to turn a hot dog van over with a person inside it, came out of the toilets. I grabbed him by the bollocks and started play-fighting and wrestling with him, and the others obviously thought, If he knows them they must be okay. It was a close thing.

On another occasion I was standing outside the main entrance to the Wolves football ground, amongst a group of fans who had said that they were going to pull a mounted officer from his horse. Suddenly the Operational Support Unit waded in and I was hit with a truncheon. The officer got a shock when I rang him and asked him for a witness statement. Then there was the time we were travelling by train up North, standing next to three lads in a corridor who had said that they were going to wreck the train toilet. My old MSU Public Order Unit was on the train escort, and as they passed through one of them spoke to me. He instantly realised that he had dropped a clanger and walked off. Fortunately the three lads didn't pick up on it.

We were encouraged to look for some new targets in Gornal and I decided to visit a pub which had been named on the way home. I walked up to the bar to order a pint and found myself in the middle of a crowd who were talking openly about what they were going to get up to at Hartlepool when they visited the so-called 'Monkey Hangers'. They were literally shouting over the top of my head and it was all useful stuff for the team. After the undercover part of the operation finished, I found myself at a police station one day interviewing one of them. He said that apparently there was a copper in the pub listening to them and when I told him it was me he had a shock.

At the end of the operation, I gave evidence for several days at Wolverhampton Crown Court. I finished on one day little knowing that the next day I would be back in the witness box giving evidence with a black eye. I went into a local pub after court for a pint and as I went to the bar a guy approached me, swearing. I ignored him but as I went to order a drink he nutted me several times and for a few moments I saw stars in front of my eyes. The pub gaffer and his son thought it was just two men fighting and pushed us both out of the front doors. I finished up in the roadway but I started to get the better of him and by the time the police arrived it looked as if I was attacking him. Fortunately some court staff recognised me and he was arrested for assault and got three months in prison. He had been in court that day and seen me giving evidence. He denied it but it was obviously a revenge attack.

We were at a game at Bradford when all the Wolves hooligans started flicking their lighters as a reference to the Bradford fire at the stadium. We identified one target from Kingswinford who did some damage but there was a second one, who we called 'Fingers', who we were never able to identify. When we went to court to give evidence at the trial of the first one, Fingers turned up as a witness for his friend so he got locked up as well.

In another court case, I was supposed to be corroborated by one of the police spotters, who we nicknamed 'Moley' because he wore big thick glasses, like The Simpsons cartoon character Mole Man. His eyesight was so bad that when he came into the court to give his evidence, he walked into the jury benches instead of the witness stand. It didn't bode well for supporting my evidence.

I felt physically drained at the end of the operation. I used to go home in the dark to avoid the neighbours seeing what I looked like. I stayed on the job for twelve months doing some of the background work after the arrests. I found it really hard to fit back into normal policing. That said, I would have done it again.

COVERT OFFICER MARK: I had eight years' service and a colleague put me forward to work undercover on GROWTH. I was a Wolves fan but I found that you didn't really need to know that much about the team and it wasn't difficult to start an argument about who was playing well and who wasn't. My partner didn't drink at all and used to take his beer and throw it down the toilet. They all thought he was a big man for being able to drink so much but the truth was he touched very little of it. Right at the end of the operation, he was pointed out as being a police officer and that was his last day on the job but thankfully he managed to get away from the situation. I was with him at the time but they ignored me at that point.

I had a new partner and we were in Brannigans pub and a target known as 'Escabano' came in. He had just come out of prison and some of the fans we were with went up to the bar to talk to him. They turned round after a while and started looking at us. My partner went white and got up and left – he had obviously been fingered. I was in there on my own thinking, how the hell do I get out of this. I went to a fruit machine and put some money in as they stared at me. Then I started banging and punching the machine and the doormen came and threw me out. I ran down a side street and hid behind a car as some of them came out looking for me.

On a more humorous occasion, we went to a game at Exeter with a younger crew. Whilst we were in a place having something to eat, they stole all the cutlery. There was a fight later on and one of these youngsters tried to stab an Exeter fan with a fork. The guy was wearing an Aran woolly jumper and as the fork got caught up in the wool, the jumper started unravelling. Everybody burst out laughing. On another occasion we went to Torquay to an away game. The police were stopping anyone with a Black Country accent from coming into the town but we were given a route to take and actually finished up having a pint with some Torquay players the night before. The night porter at the place we stayed at was a reformed alcoholic who looked after us well.

The main guys were very well organised. You could see them on phones, arranging fights. Sometimes some of the older ones would tell us where to go for a safe drink. We didn't usually wear colours but when we were up in Hartlepool a local fan 'made' us and punched my partner for no reason. We would have let it go but it was witnessed, so we finished up with another court appearance at Middlesbrough Crown Court.

In one incident an officer videoed a group of fans trying to push an opposing fan's head under the wheels of a taxi near to the bridge on Wolverhampton railway station. Those were the moments that you realised that this was a serious business we were involved in.

For me it was a job well done, with more than one hundred arrests. I was really proud to have been on it. After the court cases, I was in a pub in Stourton one day, off duty, when about ten hooligans who had been sent down on GROWTH came into the bar and recognised me straight away. They came up to me and said that they would 'see me out on the car park'. Some of the locals got wind of what was happening and I was told not to get involved. A group of them went outside and 'sorted' them out whilst I finished my drink. They were told not to come back!

CHAPTER 15

AFTERMATH

O NE SUNDAY LUNCHTIME in November 1987, the team
met in a quiet back-street hostelry in Birmingham city
centre, not far from Steelhouse Lane Police Station. The
Gunmakers was a pub often used by officers in those days. The
place was ruled by an Irish landlady who seemed a tough old
sort but had an inner warmth, which made her a match for
virtually any situation as well as a perfect innkeeper. When
we went for a drink we wanted to relax and simply be able to
be ourselves, and for that The Gunmakers was ideal. We had
used another 'safe' pub on occasions before: the Hereford in
Kyrwicks Lane, Sparkbrook, also down a back street. Everyone
in The Gunmakers knew who we were but we were left alone
and as the pub closed in the middle of that afternoon – as they
were required to do then – we remained behind to share our
last moments as a team together. Outside it was clear and sunny
and inside the atmosphere was good too, but with no great celebration or frivolity, just a feeling of quiet satisfaction and sense
of achievement at having done something good for our city.

A few of the officers there had been involved in the arrest-
planning phase. There were a few family members too, as

well as Danny and Don, the undercover officers who had returned to normal duties after the tense stand-off in The Crown. Nobody was being judged on their individual contribution and no one was trying to claim too much credit, we all knew who had placed themselves fully in harm's way for a team result and those who had been more cautious in their contribution to the cause. In one way or another, for those few relaxing hours, we were truly just a small band of brothers; the details didn't matter.

I have never been a heavy drinker, despite being a career detective, and the afternoon remained a fairly sedate affair for me. There were no formalities or formal speeches but no riotous behaviour either. I wanted it to be that way. This did not prevent the team from presenting me with a spoof folder entitled Mad Mick, which I of course accepted with good grace. The file listed my activities, such as wandering around Hill Street and Birmingham city centre hoping and looking for trouble, having secret meetings in The Hereford pub and frequently attending football matches. It itemised various 'offences' I had committed, such as failing to maintain a sense of humour, having a 'head loss' over the removal of marker pens, constant writing on notice boards, persistent statement making and over-reacting to my papers and desk being moved. For such matters I was bound over and restricted to telephone the office only once a day whilst off duty. It was all police humour, with no offence intended and certainly none taken!

By early evening, people were beginning to leave The Gunmakers. I said goodbye to each officer and wished them well, knowing which ones disliked me for the way I had made them work so hard, and which ones would be there to work for me again in the future. Nothing was said in this regard but everyone knew their stance. I knew that they had all been affected by the experience in some way, as indeed had I, and that not all of it had been positive. Most of them had enjoyed the freedom of undercover and covert work and I could see already that fitting them back into a uniformed, disciplined organisation might prove difficult. There had no doubt been a sense of elation at the end of Operation Red Card's arrest phase but for some this was followed by a sense of loss and purpose as they shifted back towards conventional policing. Whatever the job or work, after the euphoria comes a form of hangover, as the return to normality brings a dip in excitement and in the feeling of importance.

At the end of the evening I stood outside for a few moments, satisfied that the gathering had gone well and that, with the finish of the operation, another line had been drawn. We had been able to pass our experiences on to the Wolverhampton officers involved in Operation GROWTH and also to officers from Manchester who ran a couple of undercover operations. I was pleased we were able to do this, to pass on proven successful advice. And of course it was a pleasant feeling to know that we had been the first to achieve such high success. Now we all needed to look towards our own futures. Whilst I wondered what mine might be, I felt happy and confident.

On 26 November, I went with my chief superintendent to a Police Committee meeting at West Midlands Police head-quarters, where a presentation was given on Red Card. The

Chief Constable was politically answerable for the performance of the force to the members of this committee, a mixture of magistrates, independents and local politicians from all parties. They were a powerful group and it was important the presentation went well. Pleasingly, it did, and the operation was subsequently also brought to the attention of the then Home Secretary, Douglas Hurd.

On 21 December, I had a meeting with the Crown Prosecution Service to discuss the progress of the files. Things were going according to plan and I had no concerns. The next day I attended the BTP Christmas function, and on the evening after that I went to the Force Intelligence CID Christmas party at the Old Royal pub in Birmingham city centre. It had been a great year overall and I enjoyed the festive atmosphere. As usual I kept a low profile and just soaked in the atmosphere. I neither sought nor wanted to be the centre of attention and there was never a shortage of people who could attract a crowd when in drink.

Dealing with the Zulu Warriors had not been an easy experience but I knew that the decision I had taken to try to remove both root and branches had been the right one. Over the years this has been translated into other versions of policing such as 'zero tolerance' but I believe that you cannot allow an 'up and comer', like one of the B Team for instance, to grow into a mainstream hooligan if it can be helped. A prime example of this was the seventeen-year-old who we nicknamed Elm due to his being tall, thin and gangly. He became relatively close to two of the undercover officers, who developed some sympathy for him as he was a likeable character and wanted friendship.

It had been clear to us that he was desperate to belong to the Zulus and this undoubtedly was a main reason for him joining in the very serious Hill Street incident. He unknowingly provided useful cover to our covert officers in much the same way as Bruno had when supporting them during the tense stand-off in The Crown, and they developed some sympathy for his naivety. As I did with Bruno, I insisted that Elm would and should have his day in court and we could only hope that he would change direction whilst he had the chance. I remained true to this approach throughout my police service and it often brought me into conflict with colleagues who only wanted to go for the big fish.

We had inflicted great damage on the Zulu Warriors and had stripped away some of their feelings of invincibility, as well as their sense of anonymity. However, I also knew that a mortal blow to the gang had not been struck: they would be back. Indeed, I was acutely aware that other elements of the hardcore Zulus had not come to our attention during Red Card, with some leaders serving prison sentences at the time for other unrelated matters or having simply got lucky and not been on our radar. Cuddles, for example, who was renowned as the figurehead of the gang, had slipped the net. To some extent, some of the leaders we did catch had simply been care-taking the roles and paid the price for it.

On 1 May 1990, at the Tally Ho Police Training Centre and in the same room in which we had held the main briefing for Red Card, I was awarded a Police Authority Commendation, together with the rest of the operational team, by the chairman of the Police Authority, for outstanding professional conduct.

It was the highest internal Force award that could be granted and came with a badge which you could, if you so wished, wear on the sleeve of your uniform as a visible symbol. It was our own Rorke's Drift moment, with the added bonus of not having to suffer any posthumous honours! The following day, in the Birmingham Evening Mail, a photograph appeared of myself and some members of the team on the night of the awards ceremony. Paul Leopold, at that point the Acting Chief Constable, said, 'I am very proud of the men who saw off football hooliganism in the West Midlands. At times they were acting under extreme danger but they kept their calm and achieved arrests to become a credit to the Force.' Significantly, the photograph featured three of the undercover officers... published with their knowledge and consent, although on reflection this was a mistake. By then I was a detective inspector in the Force Intelligence Department, so the badge would have to wait, but in due course, when I was promoted again into uniform some years later, it was sewn on and worn with pride.

*

The following retrospective comments come from officers involved in Operation Red Card. Alex was the only one of our covert officers to go on further undercover assignments despite the fact that he was not particularly attracted to the work. He and I gave talks to the first ever course for undercover officers in the West Midlands the year after Operation Red Card.

ALEX: After the job finished I went back to the Operational Support Unit and then the D Division. I used to do the occasional spotting for Villa and the Blues but no-one ever recognised me. At one point I was on a raid at the Elmdon Club next to Birmingham Airport and Elm was there. I stood right next to him but he didn't recognise me.

LIAM: Just after Red Card I was out with my chief inspector from the Operational Support Unit. Blues were playing Villa at Villa Park. After the game, the two of us got stuck in Witton Lane and were isolated, with Villa on one side and Blues on the other. The chief inspector said, 'What do we do now?' I said 'With respect, Sir, get your truncheon out, be aggressive and shout at them, and pray.' We did exactly that and got away with it. Afterwards he said it was great fun apart from nearly 'shitting himself'.

I made about one hundred and fifty public order arrests in less than four years on the OSU but could never understand why grown men could behave like animals. I went on to do a lot of spotting for Villa over the next twelve years and compiled a book on all the main targets, with black and white photos of them. We learnt a lot on Operation Red Card and I tried to put this to good use.

Undercover officer Adam retired at detective inspector level in the Force Intelligence Department after thirty years' service and having spent a long time as a supervisor on the Firearms Department.

ADAM: I was never seriously affected by it all. I was frustrated at times because we were not at the forefront of some of the major incidents. We tried hard to be but were unlucky. We were in the swing of it and I would have liked to have gone on. Our exit strategy was to finish the operation on the Friday and start arresting people again in uniform on the Monday but with less daytime drinking! When I finished I was posted to Uniform Charlie Serial on the OSU. My sergeant on the serial, Pete, said we should do a walk-through of The Crown. It was not my idea. The first Saturday I was back working I had my hair cut and the whole serial ten of us went in there. The barmaid made eye contact with me. Her mouth dropped open. There were only a few in there and no one of interest. It was probably the last time I went into the place. Not long after going back I was promoted to sergeant and went to Thornhill Road.

Lee retired from the West Midlands Police with thirty years' service after spending his last nine years on the Central Motorway Patrol Group. He is still serving as a police officer in a British overseas territory and amongst his duties he is a dedicated wildlife officer, a family liaison officer and an authorised firearms officer. He remains committed to the job.

LEE: I was and still am very proud to have been involved in the job. It was a clean job with no issues and lots of guilty pleas. I still remember it well and for months used to spend time thinking about how I might have done things better. There wasn't a day before a match when I wasn't physically sick beforehand. I could actually be sick on the way to The Crown without losing my stride. What pissed me off though were the ones who we didn't manage to get and I would have liked to have kept going longer.

COLIN: At the end of the job I went back on the OSU in uniform. Psychologically it was very hard to adjust at first, going back into some of these places in uniform. I have thought about it over the years. Once you have experienced something like that it never leaves you. Now that I am older and wiser and have more experience, if I was asked again I would say, 'No.' Equally I was very proud to have been part of it. The testimony is that twenty-seven years on we can still remember big chunks of it and the camaraderie that was being developed amongst our team without us really knowing about it.

The level of violence that they were prepared to use has never ceased to amaze me. If you asked the Zulus today what their thoughts would be, with many of them in their fifties now, would they have the same feelings?

I retired after thirty years' service in the rank of detective inspector. I last saw service working on covert and international policing issues for a national government agency. I am a Manchester United fan and was a season ticket holder at Old Trafford for years. Birmingham City is my second team and I love football. I am currently qualified as a professional football coach and oversee a semi-professional development centre for youth football.

BARRIE DAVIES: I was a Blues fan. I cannot be a hundred per cent sure that it was Francis, but in about 1990 I was in the seats for the Birmingham v Carlisle FA Autoglass Final at Wembley Stadium, with my father, when a West Indian male came over to me and said, 'Hello, Mister Davies, do you remember me, you arrested me on the football job?' It was half-time. We exchanged pleasantries and shook hands and that was it. This was part of the culture: on the one hand they hated us but they also respected who we were and knew that we had dealt with them properly.

ANDY MURCOTT, who would retire as an inspector after thirty years' service: This was the largest investigation I was ever involved in and I remember the amount of work involved in preparing the case papers. I also remember the close liaison we had with the CPS and the meetings we had with Desmond Jaggers. Although we had our share of arguments, I remember it being a really good team effort. The hardcore Zulus were up for a fight and they knew that they were putting their lives on the line, yet they did it. In that sense they were not cowards. The sentences for our main protagonists were slightly disappointing but the operation was a huge success and represented the end of the road for the Zulu Warriors, for the time being. I am very proud of what we achieved.

Steve Trenbirth retired as a detective sergeant with West Midlands Police and was an expert on major incident room procedures. He was born in Erdington to the sound of Villa Park and has remained a supporter of Aston Villa.

STEVE TRENBIRTH: Years after Operation Red Card, I went away for a long weekend with my wife and stayed at a hotel. There was a white guy in his twenties there with his partner. We got chatting and I disclosed that I was a police officer. He was a bit frosty towards me at first but as we chatted over a drink he told me that he was a Birmingham City supporter and that he had been a serious hooligan. We hadn't arrested him on Red Card but he said that he knew that he had been targeted by the police. He said that he got 'a real high' from it all and that as far as he was concerned it was fine to carry a blade and that whilst you could slash the face or the body of your opponent, you never went for the neck because a cut to the jugular could leave you facing a murder charge. He was fine to chat to but he wasn't the sort of person you would want to cross.

I was pleased I worked with Operation Red Card because it was an experience that I would not have got anywhere else. Having said that, I used to like doing jobs that you moved on quickly from day to day. Because this went on for months, it did get me down a bit at times.

*

The antics of the Zulu Warriors were now a part of Birmingham's history – a particularly disreputable part, it has to be said – and would continue to affect the community in the city in unforeseen ways. One of these was a controversy in 1987, the year of Operation Red Card, over the police commissioning a commemorative painting of the

1985 Birmingham City soccer riot in which a thirteen-year-old boy was killed, one of the worst disturbances ever at a British soccer game. The West Midlands Police Federation paid artist John Edwards to paint a riot scene showing a charging white police horse being stoned at St Andrew's. Chief Constable Mr Geoffrey Dear agreed to autograph a limited edition of 250 prints taken from the painting. The prints were sold for £35 each, with all proceeds going to the Police Convalescent Home charity fund. 'The picture shows a turning point in the history of West Midlands Police in the new level of violence which they were expected to cope with – without any increase in manning levels or equipment,' a police spokesman told the press.

Not everyone was happy with the idea. 'We are trying to forget what happened and this is serving to revive bad memories,' said Birmingham City's club secretary, John Westmancoat. 'It is for a good cause but I am rather surprised that the police should see fit to do this sort of thing.' Officials from Handsworth's Afro Caribbean Resource Centre went further, claiming the painting was insulting and that it suggested that black youths were solely responsible for the violence. It depicted a number of black youths, including one with a stone in his hand, close to the horse at the height of the disturbances. 'Someone must have instructed the painter that this was the type of painting they would like the public to see,' a spokesman for the centre was quoted as saying. 'If that was printed or pasted up on the community walls or notice boards it could in itself cause a riot.' West Midlands Police responded that the painting, called A Different Ball Game, had been taken from video recordings and the depiction of the black youths was coincidental.

Speaking as a former police officer, I felt that the painting was relevant, portraying an event that stretched the ethos of the 'thin blue line' to the limit. The officer on the white horse epitomised this by charging into the middle of the crowd and to some extent turning the tide, almost another Rorke's Drift moment, with a few officers refusing to run from a horde of attackers. This is why the white horse takes centre stage in the picture. There were political messages in the responses by both the football club and the police. One was about trying to repair a tarnished image and the other was about highlighting shortages of manpower and equipment. The picture was and is emotive. It also clearly shows both black and white youths attacking the police, reinforcing the image of the Zulus as a multiracial group.

Personally, I like the painting, partly because it is a reminder of that Leeds game, bearing in mind that following the Red Card arrests we were able to prove that some of the targets were there in 1985. In other words, it helped reiterate the significance of hooliganism to the city and to bring the event forward into 1987, a highly important time for the police force's continuing battle against the football thugs. I don't think it is wrong to voice differing opinions about the painting as, clearly, viewing it through the eyes of a football supporter it is easy to see how one might feel it to be insensitive. But the poor boy that died was not involved on the pitch and the painting does not refer to the tragedy of his death. The picture is complex because it celebrates acts of bravery versus mindless acts of hatred carried out in the name of a sport. Playing devil's advocate, it also records a moment in time when the police lost control – and that is one step away from anarchy.

EPILOGUE

IN THE SUMMER of 1988, I was promoted to the rank of inspector in uniform at Sutton Coldfield Police Station. This was situated on the 'D' Division of the force area and whilst it included the fairly affluent area of Sutton Coldfield it also covered Castle Vale, which suffered from social deprivation and high crime levels. Much of the crime was connected to one well-known local family. During my first meeting with my new superintendent, I was told that I would be taking over one of the less successful units. I was far from satisfied with that description and so planned accordingly. Six months later, he attended one of our morning parades and told my unit that they were the best. They were indeed the best, they just hadn't known it before. They had needed help, encouragement, strong leadership and management.

The division also covered the Villa Park football ground and I had the 'pleasure' of performing duties in uniform there on two occasions, both of which finished up with me getting involved in disturbances. I always much preferred to watch any action on the terraces than that on the pitch and on the first occasion I was walking around one of the home terraces with an officer when a steward approached us for help. He had a problem with a youth sitting on top of a concrete pillar near to an exit point. What started off for us as a fairly simple issue developed quickly into a stand-off. Despite our reasonable requests for him to come down, the youth responded with a hard stare and a challenge: 'Make me.' Many of the crowd around us were taking a more than casual interest in the situation and I realised that our approach needed to change; the time for negotiation was at an end. And so, as one, my colleague and I pulled the youth down and arrested him for a public order offence. He did not fight but he refused to be compliant and we virtually had to drag him several hundred yards to the police detention room, where some of the officers looked on with curiosity because inspectors did not normally involve themselves in arrests. Given the choice, neither would I; I was exhausted after those particular exertions!

The second incident again occurred with a single officer and I in an area below the stands. Two Villa fans were verbally abusing visiting supporters and despite warnings they continued. So we took one each and arrested them for threatening behaviour. They both struggled and began calling on people around us to help them. We called for our own assistance on the radio and began to edge back into a corner with our backs to a wall and our prisoners secured in front of us. The crowd around us was becoming more and more volatile and a few of them aimed punches our way or tried to pull the two yobs away from us, but with their bodies between us and the crowd, the prisoners actually copped the worst of it.

The truth is, we were not going to give them up, the unwritten rule being that once you made an arrest you never let your prisoner go willingly. That would have been an unforgivable display of weakness and loss of face. When you are in such situations, time appears to pass very slowly and you just pray and try to grow six inches taller and wider! In those days we still carried wooden truncheons in a long, sewn-in pocket in the right trouser leg but I didn't draw mine. Those truncheons were next to useless and the problem was that if you did draw one then you stood the real risk of having it wrenched from you and then used against you. The only time I ever used mine was in 1972 when I was part of a travelling BTP serial escorting a 'football special' train. As we left London, bricks were thrown at us and a carriage window smashed. I used my truncheon to knock out some of the exposed pieces of glass.

Finally, after what seemed ages but in reality was a few minutes, the 'cavalry' surged through the crowd and rescued us. Once the odds had evened up, nobody else wanted 'to play' any more and our prisoners were quickly secured. The crowd's actions merely confirmed my long-held view that most people who inflict violence are inherently cowards, particularly in group situations. Sweating and exhausted again, I resolved to make sure that this did not become a regular practice. In those days, because of the activities of hooligan groups the focus of the football clubs and the police was still very much on crowd segregation and literally fencing people in, thus addressing public order but with public safety being a secondary issue. Little did we know at the time how those principles would reverse themselves in the future as a result of a tragic event that touched us all: Hillsborough.

*

During the last few months of my police service – I was nearing retirement – I again stood on New Street Station in Birmingham in 2011 in full uniform. I had by this time dropped down in rank to work as a superintendent with the British Transport Police, the force I had started with all those years ago in September 1968. Standing next to me, also in uniform, was a fellow BTP officer, James, one of the covert officers who had worked on Operation Red Card with me, replacing one of the 'accused' coverts. He had maintained an interest throughout his career in football intelligence and was an expert in his field whilst I had gone on to become a chief superintendent. He was an extremely loyal individual whom I had maintained contact with over the years, and he was still a fanatical Aston Villa supporter. He was to be at my wedding in 2012; it wasn't just the Zulu Warriors who could have lifelong friendships. And here we were years later, still totally anonymous to this group.

New Street Station was familiar territory for me and I loved the feel of the transient population and changing environment. I felt almost at home. I had started my police service as a Police Cadet with the BTP in Birmingham and knew every inch of this place and the tricks that were played by the people who used it. On one particular Saturday morning all those years ago, I recall watching the antics of the younger supporters who would go and buy child tickets for their mates, who should have paid full price. It gave them credibility with the older ones but this day was not to be theirs. I 'clocked' the faces of several and the train they were going on, and then called up the BTP officers from the office, who came down with me to the platform. The fans were lined up and dealt with for ticket fraud. They were not a happy bunch of supporters, because they didn't go to the match, and not a happy bunch of police officers, because I had given them some work to do! I didn't win any popularity prizes that day but I considered it great fun and had no intention of changing my ways.

In 2011, I was there for the derby match between Birmingham City and Aston Villa, always a grudge encounter, on and off the pitch. On the station concourse were gathered some of the old and not so old faithful supporters, traditional Bluenoses mixed with the old Zulu Warrior vanguard. They were out today to show their Villa rivals that they were still a force to reckon with. I travelled on the train with them and their police escort. They didn't know me and would have been surprised to hear of the part I had played in their short but eventful history. They showed no animosity towards the police on this day, other than one idiot who had drunk too much and insisted on letting us know his views of the world. But I knew that little had changed and I knew what was coming. Our older generation of Zulus looked on with amuse-ment but made no effort to get involved as we encouraged him to quieten down. Such behaviour was simply beneath them. Policing trains is an entirely different style to that of policing the streets. You have to work in confined conditions, in close proximity to potential offenders, with nowhere to go and no immediate prospects of assistance if you get into trouble. We, however, were 'old school' too and well versed in the art of positive communication. He decided to shut up and the journey concluded without incident, although we felt sure there would be plenty in store as the day went on.

We arrived at Witton Railway Station and the fans massed together with a sense of anticipation for the short walk to the Villa ground, escorted by West Midlands Police. I stood at the station and waited. I was nearly at the end of my police career and to some extent this was a day of great nostalgia for me. However, I knew what was coming. Five minutes later and the familiar sounds of the police sirens started. The Zulu Warriors were writing another page in their history and in a quirky sort of way I felt almost privileged to have been present, although I still abhorred violence. People sometimes asked me which team I supported and although I supported no-one, if pushed for an answer I would reluctantly admit to having an affinity to Birmingham City. I was certainly not a Villa fan like my colleague James.

*

April 2012 saw me sitting in the altogether more pleasant surroundings of the Aperitivo Restaurant in Nicosia, Cyprus, with my wife, Andry, and a football intelligence officer by the name of Michalis from the Republic of Cyprus Police. Here we were, some twenty-five years after Operation Red Card, discussing football hooliganism in an informal setting and with the sun shining, over 2,000 miles away from Birmingham. We talked specifically about extreme violence between the football hooligans in Cyprus, amongst supporters of the teams Omonoia, Apollon, AEL, Anorthosis and Apoel, from Nicosia and Limassol. It might not be well-known in Britain but the problem in Cyprus is acute, with major incidents spanning two decades. In one incident, a marine flare was lit and thrown into a car with two people inside whilst the doors were held shut; they were lucky to survive. Assaults on police officers were routine and in one case an officer died of a heart attack during disturbances. Sticks, stones, bottles, flares, iron bars and Molotov cocktails were commonplace weapons. It was out of hand and the politicians, police and clubs seemed unable to act jointly to stop it.

Back home, Birmingham City supporters had still featured heavily in the arrest figures for the BTP at the end of the previous season but they no longer regularly turned out a hardcore group of dedicated thugs, now commonly referred to as 'risk supporters', on the rail network. I had retained my interest in football violence during the previous two years and we had adopted a very firm approach to policing this issue.

In Nicosia we discussed CCTV, spotters, intelligence from evidence-gathering teams, stewarding and undercover work. With a local population of less than a million people, where everyone knows just about everyone else, and with legislation that differed from the UK, it was clear that they faced real challenges in ever mounting the kind of operation I had. I sympathised with Michalis but also felt frustrated: here was another opportunity to make a difference and I was not going to be part of it. I stressed that I believed football violence could never be totally eradicated but that I was convinced that with good intelligence and operational planning it could be controlled and significantly reduced. I believe that I illustrated this when conducting other football-related operations in the years following Red Card. In May and July 2014, I worked with reporters from the Cyprus Mail to produce two front-page newspaper articles on the problems they faced and offered a number of solutions.

Looking back over the years, we were effectively just amateurs in terms of the world of undercover policing but we proved that it could work. I believe this provided confidence to others to move forward in this specialised and highly dangerous field of expertise. I was and remain convinced that once you remove the veil of anonymity from the people involved and they know that they run the risk of being arrested, then you start to change their mentality. After Red Card, the Zulu Warriors who we arrested, or their associates, remained on stringent bail conditions for some months with the threat of bail being withdrawn if they breached them. Those who had not been arrested were looking over their shoulders for some time afterwards. The hunters had become the hunted and they knew it was time to change their habits.

I wished Michalis the best of luck, little knowing then that I would later decide to chart the history of hooliganism in Cyprus, leading me to write an ebook, Violence in the Sun: A History of Football Hooliganism in Cyprus. You never know what life will throw up, do you?

In 2013, I met a detective inspector from West Midlands Police who was part of an investigation team looking at the history of covert policing. Operation Red Card has a place in that history. What I had not fully appreciated before was that it was used as a springboard to establish a full-time undercover unit to look at all aspects of crime. I believe that the DI was genuinely surprised at the degree of planning and thoroughness in our 1987 operation. Even after all those years, it gave me cause for quiet satisfaction.

I recently saw One-Eyed Baz on a television programme. When discussing his past exploits with the Zulus, he said, 'The biggest firm is the police. You will never beat them, will you?' He was right.

ACKNOWLEDGMENTS

Michael Layton would like to thank the Red Card team, and former colleagues, for letting me back into their lives and for their valuable insight; Birmingham Central Library (Archive Section), the Birmingham *Evening Mail* and the *Sunday Mercury*; and above all my wife Andry, for her patience and support.

Robert Endeacott would like to thank Ray Allen, Vincent Bull, Michael Hodges, Les Johnson, Robert Law and Steven Morgan-Vandome, and to acknowledge the authors of *Birmingham In The 70s and 80s*, by Alton and Jo Douglas (Brewin Books), and *Zulus*, by Caroline Gall (Milo Books), for their valuable work

Printed in Great Britain
by Amazon